what others are saying about
FIND YOUR FIRE AT FORTY

Find Your Fire at Forty takes us way beyond the boundaries of a 5-step process to improvement, placing you (through your imagination) as one of the characters in the story. This book will take you there! You will find your fire, learn how you can dissipate your limitations and create your life on purpose. This book is as much a guide as it is a gift.

—DAVID ASARNOW, *www.WakeUpAndLiveRich.com*

In today's culture, adults can find life's transition when we get into our forties challenging. *Find Your Fire at Forty* takes the reader on a journey through this transition with practical tips on the key factors to understand. The stories that Heather Hansen O'Neill shares helps the reader relate to her message. I would highly recommend this book for anyone dealing with what can be a very fearful time in everyone's life.

—**TIM KELLIS**, *Author of* Equality: The Quest for the Happy Marriage

Find Your Fire at Forty is compelling and insightful. Not only will you be inspired to take your life to the next level, you are given a 5-step action plan to accomplish it. It's a must read!

—**HARV EKER**, *Author of the #1 NY Times Bestseller* Secrets of the Millionaire Mind

This remarkable and readable book is a tantalizing look at the reality that life offers us. With a great sense of humor and an understanding heart Heather has created a valuable guide to anyone who has moved through their life and is asking the simple yet mysterious question; WHO AM I NOW? Heather is a fabulous human being and outstanding mentor who continues to help many people with their personal growth as they begin to rediscover their own true essence. This is an intriguing tool and guide that will have you remembering and experiencing who you really are and taking steps to once again living your life full out.

—**GAIL VILCU**, *Greater Vision Coaching and Training*

Riveting! You won't be able to put *Find Your Fire at Forty* down. It's the recipe for breaking through and closing the gap from where you are to where you want to be.

—**CROIX SATHER**, *the man who ran across America to inspire a nation, and author of* Dream Big Act Big.

FIND YOUR FIRE AT FORTY

CREATING A *Joyful* LIFE DURING THE AGE OF DISCONTENT

HEATHER HANSEN O'NEILL

MORGAN JAMES PUBLISHING • NEW YORK

FIND YOUR FIRE AT FORTY

ISBN: 978-1-60037-846-1 (Paperback)
Library of Congress Control Number: 2010933818

Published by:
MORGAN JAMES PUBLISHING
1225 Franklin Ave Ste 32
Garden City, NY 11530-1693
Toll Free 800-485-4943
www.MorganJamesPublishing.com

Cover/Interior Design by:
Rachel Lopez
rachel@r2cdesign.com

contents

preface

Are you discontent with any portion of your life? Do you find yourself wanting more?

Often we spend the first part of our lives striving to reach goals that may or may not have been forced upon us. We work, care for family, and constantly strive to fulfill our numerous obligations. Then at some point we wake up and ask "Is this all there is?"

Find Your Fire at Forty: Creating a Joyful Life During the Age of Discontent provides an innovative look at how to transition through pain and discontent to a more productive, joyful life. The lessons are based upon the five step process of my Fire in Five speaking and coaching program. It stems from a compilation of personal experience, interviews of people in middle age that have successfully transitioned through pain and discontent, and practical, proven strategies.

The goal of *Find Your Fire at Forty: Creating a Joyful Life During the Age of Discontent* is to inspire readers to step outside their comfort zone, align themselves with their own truth, live more passionately, find what they are uniquely qualified to do, and learn how to use that talent to serve the world.

This book begins as a story, with characters based upon real people who have been interviewed. Its message allows you to connect and empathize with the characters' vulnerabilities and progression.

The second part of the book is a concise breakdown of the five step process to joyful living. Research, true stories, and an easy to follow guideline provide clear recommendations while excerpts from the story illustrate how the process works. This combination makes it easy for you to walk away with an action plan for success.

I'd like to thank my clients and interviewees that graciously shared their stories. To protect confidentiality, all names have been changed.

I appreciate the many friends and family members that have continually supported me in my journeys.

BOOK 1 :

THE CONVERSATION

What a day! He was on top of the world. Jenny McAllister asked to sit next to him at the assembly. She even offered to share her candy. He couldn't believe his luck.

Jenny McAllister with the big, blue eyes and the golden hair so long and straight she could tie it in a knot.

His excitement spurred his feet to speed. He couldn't wait to tell the man. He opened the door but before he could call out the hair on his arms stood on end. Something was wrong. Still as a statue he waited, dread dripping over him like molasses.

He climbed the stairs one cautious step at a time until he heard the gurgling. That sound lit a fire under his feet and he ran through the house searching.

On the second floor he saw the man's body…convulsing. The man was staring at him or through him, he couldn't be sure. He shrieked, "Help! What can I do?"

The man grabbed the boy's arm. Trying to rip the vice like fingers from his wrist, the boy watched the life seep from the man's eyes…and he screamed.

Grasping his sheet as if it were a life raft, Noor awoke sweaty and breathless. After a few moments his breathing returned to normal and he attempted to shake the dream out of his head. It was never that easy. These nightmares were becoming more and more frequent. What does it mean? He'd have to talk to the doctor about it.

He threw his legs over the bed and searched for his workout shorts. Banana eaten, water drank, legs stretched, and laces tied…he was ready.

His favorite part of running was working through the pain in his legs and tightness in his chest, feeling the sweat drip from his brow, wanting to stop but not…experiencing the loosening of muscles and the freedom of his body responding to his will.

Returning home he showered and prepared for the day. Noor was invigorated and ready to spend some time with his friends at the Coffee Encounter.

But first, an hour of study…the teacher must remain the student.

chapter 1

Opening

It was a brisk March morning and the city held an energy that made one quicken his pace in anticipation. Pea coats were flapping but the blue sky and golden sun created an air of optimism never found in the depths of January.

Tucked away on a midtown side street was a coffee shop like no other. At first glance, it appeared remote and ordinary. Upon entering, warmth filled the customers imploring them to stay for a time. Rarely did anyone decide to take their coffee to go.

Erin looked over her shoulder as she walked into Coffee Encounter. What on earth was she thinking coming here again? Paul would kill her if he found out.

Paul hated places like this. He didn't like being around strangers and he complained about spending a fortune on coffee that could melt a spoon. Erin loved Coffee Encounter, with the oversized comfy chairs so lived in she felt like she was getting a hug, and the captivating artwork that changed each week so the patrons could enjoy various artists' styles. The newest artwork was a bit odd but Erin liked unusual art and the one by the restroom was colorful and engaging as if a seven year old had drawn it with colored pencils.

Erin could get lost here. People were engrossed in their conversations and no one seemed to mind Erin becoming engrossed in her reading. Behind the counter she saw the cute guy whose nametag read, "Hi, my name is Noor. How can I get you going this morning?" He put aside his reading and gave her that lopsided grin that made Erin blush.

"Hi, Erin. What are you reading today? No, no don't tell me. Something romantic, right?"

"Not today, Noor. I needed a chuckle so I brought a Chelsea Handler selection."

"How very decadent of you! I approve."

"Thanks. What's your book today?"

"I'm rereading my grandfather's autobiography. He was an amazing man. If I can make half the impact on the world that he did then I would be happy."

"What do you like best about it?"

"It's in his voice. He wrote like he lived. Family and friends were very important to him and he always followed through. The stories in his book bring me closer to him because I can feel the faith he had in humankind and God."

"That's beautiful. May I borrow it when you finish?"

"Of course. I think you'll like it. What can I get you?"

She ordered her no fat latte, paid with exact change and made her way to a table by the window. Opening her book with a sigh, this was her one moment today to feel content.

Edward watched the beautiful redhead sit at her usual window table. He had seen her many times before and every time she caught his attention. He wondered why she worked so hard at avoiding eye contact.

He grinned as he thought of how much he loved connecting with people and discussing current events here with opinionated coffee drinkers. The redhead looked smart and might be up for a good debate if he could get her to look up.

What book did she have this time? Edward couldn't tell by the way she was holding it however he was certain he hadn't read it anyway. If it wasn't about making money he wouldn't touch it.

Something about her made him want to reach out. There was a sadness in her that made him want to protect her. How strange to feel that way about someone he had never even spoken to.

Glancing at his phone, Edward realized it was time to go. He jumped back into work mode and became energized thinking about his afternoon meeting. The exhilaration of being the go-to guy for his clients' financial success made him feel powerful and worthwhile.

Completely out of his comfort zone but unable to stop himself, he placed his card on the table in front of the redhead. He said, "You seem like someone I'd like to know better. Call me sometime if you want to talk." He wanted to say more but between her bright red cheeks and the surprised expression he guessed she didn't get hit on as often as he expected. Trying not to come on too strong he added, "Only if you're comfortable. I'll see you next time."

Erin felt her skin burn. The man that dropped his card was gorgeous. She's seen him here before. Tall, strong, and confident. Not an insufferable confidence that masks deficiencies, more a quiet poise born of conviction in his abilities. She took a moment to imagine his hands touching her cheek then she shook her head as if trying to push the image out. She forced her attention back on her book.

As he was leaving, Edward held the door open for the distraught mom attempting to fit through with a double stroller and a toddler. Edward walked away shaking his head remembering those days. Not that he'd ever pushed the stroller. His wife had handled the brunt of the younger years.

A momentary ache caused him to pause as he recalled Brian's sad face and plea this morning. Edward must arrange his work meetings to make it to Brian's baseball game this weekend. He missed that little dude. He made a mental note to bring his glove for some practice catches before the game.

Back in Coffee Encounter Brenda, who had entered with her three little ones, was starting to lose it, "Don't touch those Sophie. I said don't touch those!" Counting to ten in her head, Brenda experienced marginal self control.

If only Zach and Ian napped at the same time everything would be alright. This sleep deprivation was eliminating her already limited patience. Brenda recently heard part of a radio program that stated people could have psychotic breaks from lack of sleep.

All she needed was a decent night's rest and she'd be back on her game. At least that's what she kept telling herself.

Brenda wasn't used to doing anything less than perfectly. School had been painless. She'd graduated *magna cum laude* with ease. Her business decisions were spot on. Her friends were impressed by the warp speed in which she rose up the corporate ladder. And when she decided Steven should be her man, the poor boy didn't have a chance. She was at the top of her game when she turned forty and the clock that had been ticking for the last few years exploded. Buzz…time to have kids.

Sophie was almost three now and Ian and Zach turned one last month. How could raising three little beings be so much harder than running a Fortune 500 company? Brenda seriously questioned the decision she'd made to quit her job to become a full time mom. She felt like any semblance of sanity had leaked out with her amniotic fluid.

She ordered, "Hi Noor. You gotta help me out. I need warm milk poured into these two bottles, an orange juice no pulp, and a large mocha latte no whipped cream as fast as humanly possible." She paid with her credit card and glanced around the room.

She was in search of some adult conversation. The redhead deep into her book seemed like a long shot. She chose to sit next to the short, fleshy blond who gave her a sympathetic smile. Hoping to stimulate an interesting dialogue Brenda said, "Hi. How's it going? My name's Brenda. Do you have kids?"

Kristy gazed at Brenda's twins wistfully, "Yes, but they're all grown up now. Sarah got married last year and Beth is off to college. I miss them being little and needing me like yours do. Oh, sorry, hi. I'm Kristy."

"Are you kidding? You look the same age as me and your kids are grown? You must have popped them out young." Brenda shook the orange juice and tested the temperature of the milk as she continued, "Not me. I wanted it all. My career first then kids; but now I wonder if I waited too long. There are days when I have no patience for diapers and screaming." As her sons opened their mouths to scream she placed the bottles of milk in and heaved a sigh.

Brenda handed Sophie her juice and a book with a picture of a horse on the front. Sophie grabbed it and said, "I wanted the one with the kitties!"

"If you ask like a big girl I'll get it for you." Brenda said.

"Pleaaaaase…" Sophie batted her eyelashes with sweet innocence.

Brenda searched in her bag and handed Sophie the book about cats. To Kristy, "Sometimes I don't know if I'm coming or going!"

"At least you know who you are." Kristy didn't notice Brenda's incredulous look. She was lost in her thoughts. *Who the hell am I?*

Brenda came here more to talk than to listen but something about the faraway gaze in Kristy's eyes called out to her. "Is there something wrong?"

Hoping Brenda would be a sympathetic ear, Kristy burst forth like a switch went off, "My job sucks. My husband and I have nothing to talk about. I have way too much time on my hands now that the girls are out of the house. I feel invisible." Kristy suddenly understood she'd said too much. This woman was a complete stranger. She was starting to lose it.

"I couldn't help but overhearing you," chimed in the man at the next table. "But, you should be thankful. At least you have a job."

Brenda was surprised by the interruption but found the new addition to the conversation fascinating. "Eavesdropping, dear sir?"

"I'm just saying. A job you hate has to be better than no job at all. After a lifetime of loyal service, one would imagine you'd get a little more respect. A little courtesy. A little notice for god's sake. I'm just saying."

Brenda's son Zach spit up on both the double stroller and his brother Ian. Sophie screamed when she realized her new dress with the yellow bow was hit. Noor assessed the situation and then went back to reading the paper.

Brenda's laughter began as a trickle and erupted like a volcano all over the coffee house. "What a crew we make! Look at us. I'm a corporate executive completely clueless as to what to do with three small kids. And you two…are just sad!" For some bizarre reason, Brenda's blunt appraisal of the situation made everyone break down into fits of uncontrollable laughter.

Brenda cleaned up Ian and Zach and assured Sophie the stain would indeed come out of her dress. She gave Sophie a coloring book and crayons and rocked the boys' stroller back and forth gently to entice them to nap.

Kristy's laughter subsided as she wiped a tear from her eye. Turning to Brenda, "Thanks for that. I was starting to wallow. I'm having a hard time lately and I can't figure out why."

Noor came over to display several new magazines and straighten the pillows on the couch. He handed Kristy one of the magazines and said, "Great article on page 17."

"Thanks Noor. I'll check it out. You always suggest the best articles." Turning to page 17, Kristy read the title *Finding Yourself in an Empty House* and decided she would read this one when she was alone.

Brenda turned to Joe, "So what's your name?"

"Joe. Sorry I came on so strong. I do that sometimes. What's yours?"

"I'm Brenda and this is Kristy. Nice to meet you. And you never have to worry about coming on too strong with me. I'm supergirl. I have a force field that keeps other people's negativity at bay."

At first Joe thought Brenda was mocking him then he noticed the twinkle in her eye and realized she was kidding around. It struck him that there may have been other times he was quick to prejudge someone's intentions. Joe glanced up and Noor was nodding and smiling at him. He must have appeared shocked because Noor came over and whispered, "No, I can't read minds but I'm very good at reading faces."

Kristy leaned over to admire the princess picture Sophie was coloring. Sophie offered her a crayon. Swallowing a lump in her throat Kristy took the crayon and worked on the princess shoes.

Knowing Brenda would have to learn this on her own Kristy ventured, "I understand these times can be overwhelming but treasure every moment. Time goes by like a flash."

"That's what everyone keeps telling me but I feel like the days are now 72 hours long." Brenda replied. As if on cue to accentuate her point Zach and Ian started crying and Sophie tugged on Brenda's shirt, "Potty Mommy. Now!"

"I'll watch the twins if you want to take your daughter to the bathroom." Kristy said.

"Thanks, that's ok. I have to wash them up anyway." She said as she headed down the hall.

"What type of work did you do, Joe?" Kristy inquired, hoping he wouldn't get mad.

"A mortgage broker. I was with the company twenty two years."

"Wow, that's a long time! You must have loved it."

Joe looked at Kristy with eyes wide and stammered, "Um. Not really…"

"Then maybe it's for the best."

With renewed conviction Joe said, "No way. They were crazy to let me go. I want to go back."

"Hmm. Well, I hope it works out for you." Kristy didn't understand why Joe would want to go back if he didn't love his job but she didn't want to press the issue. Gathering up her things, "I've got to get going but I want to say goodbye to Brenda." Kristy finished her latte and placed it in the bucket by the counter.

"Ok. Take care." Joe gave a wave then called out, "Hey Noor. One more tea please."

"Coming right up, Joe"

Brenda came out of the bathroom with the troops. Kristy waved, "Bye. Nice to meet you." Then she blew kisses to Brenda's kids.

"I'm leaving too. I'll walk out with you." As she headed for the front door Brenda said, "Bye Noor. Bye Joe. It was nice to meet you."

"Good luck, kiddo," Joe answered.

Noor waved, and then checked to see if the scones needed to be replenished.

Kristy and Brenda's conversation continued as they hiked out into the city wilderness.

chapter 2

Fear

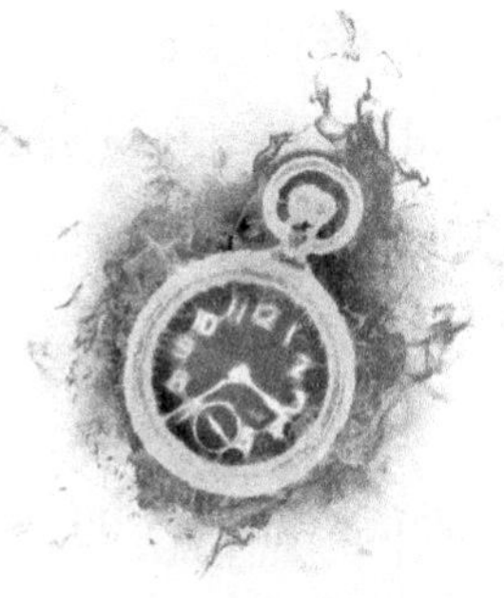

Erin:

A muscular man of average height entered Coffee Encounter. He opened the door gently but there was an intensity about him that screamed anything but gentle. Sensing his presence, Erin quickly rose from her seat and the book fell from her hand. The crack of the book slapping the floor, combined with the panic in her eyes, seemed to put Paul at ease.

Leaning in for a kiss, he said, "Hi honey. I thought I might find you here."

"I just needed a few minutes to myself before going to work. I wasn't here long."

"Now Erin, why would you need time to yourself? You have me." His grin never quite made it to his eyes. "I'll walk you to work. Nothing like time together with the one you love. Right, Babe?"

As if dodging a bullet, Erin exhaled, quickly gathered her things, and flashed him a smile. From behind the counter Noor watched Paul drape his arm over Erin's shoulder. Noor then grabbed a crumpled napkin from the counter and scribbled a note.

Paul kept his arm around Erin the entire walk to the law firm of Goldstein and Smith. She'd been working as a paralegal at the firm for the last twelve years. She liked the research, the filing, and learning about the cases. She supposed she was lucky to have a job she enjoyed but she sensed she wouldn't be here forever.

"Okay. Thanks for walking with me. I'll see you later at home. I'll make meatloaf. You like that."

"No, no, no Erin. It wouldn't be gentlemanly to drop you at the door. I'll walk you to your desk."

"That's okay. You don't have to."

"I insist," He said with no room for debate.

They went to Erin's desk on the fifth floor. Paul kissed her, a bit too passionately considering the wandering eyes of her fellow employees, and then left. Erin sunk into her chair, closed her eyes, and silently recited her mantra *I will be strong. I will be strong* to keep the tears from falling. It was working but as she opened her eyes she saw Harriet Goldstein staring down at her. Sitting up abruptly, "I'm sorry, Ms. Goldstein. Was there something you needed?"

"Erin, what the hell do you see in that guy?"

"Oh, he's okay. He just has a lot on his mind right now." Erin hurried to defend Paul as she tidied her desk.

"Don't you realize that you are smart? And talented? And you don't have to take that kind of...." Goldstein ran out of steam when she noticed

Erin getting uncomfortable, "Forgive me, it's not my business. Please have the O'Hare brief on my desk in the next ten minutes."

As Erin moved her purse to find the brief below, she saw the business card of the man from Coffee Encounter sticking out of the side pocket. She tentatively slid it out, placed it on her desk, and stared at it.

She could feel her pulse race as she lifted the receiver and dialed the number. Don't answer, don't answer, don't answer. When his voicemail stated he was out of the office, her heart dropped in disappointment. Realizing he probably had caller ID, she quickly said, "Hi. It's Erin from Coffee Encounter. Saw your card, um, I mean I know you said to call but I'm not sure why." Covering the receiver she exhaled, collected her thoughts and continued with, "If you want to reach me my number at work is 888-555-1243 extension 3. Okay. Bye." She hung up and dropped her head into her hands until her breathing was back to normal.

"Ma'am," The courier startled Erin.

"Can I help you?" She replied.

"I have an envelope for Erin Matthews. Is that you?"

Confused Erin signed the form and opened the letter.

A flyer inside announced a seminar on Wednesday at 6pm. Stapled to the flyer was a crumbled napkin with the words *Please Come to Coffee Encounter this Wednesday. It's a matter of life and death.* She suspected Noor had written the note but she could not come up with a single reason why. And why on earth would something like this be important enough to require a courier? A matter of life and death. That seemed so over the top. Suddenly she remembered, "The brief!" She placed the flyer in her top drawer, gathered up the file, and rushed over to Ms. Goldstein's office.

Edward:

Walking back to the office, Edward wondered if his assistant had printed the handouts for this afternoon's meeting. He took out his cell phone and it rang in his hand. Caller ID showed his wife Elizabeth's number. Decisions, decisions. If he blew her off she would just keep calling all day long. With a sigh he answered, "Hello Elizabeth. What's wrong?"

"What makes you think there's something wrong?"

"Usually is."

"Are you going to start on me again? After the day I've had. The painter never showed and I got a call from Brian's principal. Can you believe it? That's the third time this month! What are we going to do with that boy?"

Edward shook his head and thought *Every time. She never phones to say hello or ask about my day. There is always a problem of some sort. And she wonders why I screen her calls. Take a deep breath. Patience will get you through this faster. You can do it, Edward.* Resigned, he sweetly responded, "I'll call the painter. And don't worry about Brian. I'll talk to him when I get home."

"He'll probably be in bed by the time you get home."

"Well, what would you like me to do? I'll take care of it at breakfast, okay?"

"If you say so. See you tonight. Bye."

Edward hung up and reflected on his college days, as he often did when Elizabeth drove him crazy. He loved college. And everybody loved him. Captain of the basketball team, parties every night; what had happened? Others were often jealous of his life and he knew he should be grateful. To him everything seemed…difficult. He couldn't put his finger on it. He was restless. There had to be more.

What to do about Elizabeth? She was so cold and stressed all the time. What happened to that fun loving fireball he married?

With each step closer to the office Edward's resolve to focus on what he had to do intensified. It was time to forget distractions and get to work.

"Hello, Sir. A gentleman left this note for you. He didn't want to wait. Have a nice day!" said the doorman.

Edward responded with a pleasant nod, "Thank you, Charlie."

Sherri rushed from the elevator, "Edward, I'm so glad I caught you. We have to talk about the Gallagher meeting."

"Give me ten minutes and meet me in my office. Oh, and Sherri, please remind me to call the painter before I leave today."

As Edward entered the elevator he read the paper Charlie had handed him. It was a seminar flyer with a hand written note *Please come. It will be very revealing.* Baffled, Edward watched the elevator doors close.

Elizabeth:

Hanging up the phone, Elizabeth sank onto the couch. Talking to Edward was exhausting. She loathed sounding needy and antagonistic. That wasn't her. She couldn't figure out why every conversation lately ended in an argument.

Edward was distracted or condescending and she resorted to nagging to get his attention. She hated it. Wiping the tears of frustration from her cheek, she rose and shuffled down the hall, mentally making her list. *Apples, waffles, peanut butter, milk…*

Brenda:

Later that night, Brenda had finally gotten the kids to bed and was soaking her aching body in a warm, relaxing bubble bath. Stretching her leg in the air she felt alluring enough to call out to her husband Steve. Just in time she saw the hair on her calves that screamed, "It's been two weeks since you've had the chance to shave!"

Maybe he wouldn't notice. Oh who the hell was she kidding? She used to consider herself beautiful. She used to care enough to shave her damn legs. Where was that crazy energy she had that allowed her to get up at 5am, workout, get to the office by 7:30, work straight through until 8pm, go out to dinner, then do it all again the next day?

Ian started crying. Brenda tried to cover her ears but his little scream pierced straight through her heart. Where the hell was Steven? She quickly dried off, put on her robe and headed to the twins room before Ian could wake Zach.

She made it just in time. As she picked up Ian, Zach squirmed for a minute, then rolled over and went back to sleep. Close one. Brenda gently rocked Ian and softly sang his favorite lullaby. As she gazed down at his drooping eyelids, smelled the sweet scent of baby shampoo, and stroked his tiny little toes she realized there was nowhere else she would rather be.

It was hard being a mom. Harder than anything else she's ever had to do. Moments like this moved her. It made her appreciate what she had and also understand that it wasn't about her. Each decision she made had a consequence that extended so much farther beyond her immediate sight. She was impacting the future.

At that moment, in the rocker, Brenda knew she would be all right. If she could see the sleeping face of one of her children each evening she was convinced it would sustain her. After a very long day she finally found the peace of mind to close her eyes and drift to sleep.

Steve woke Brenda when he put Ian's sleeping body into his crib. He whispered, "Come to bed."

"I'll be in as soon as I go through the mail and load the dishwasher."

Brenda wished she could be more like Steve. She read an article about the differences between men and women. When men say they are tired they get up and go to bed. When a woman says she's tired she feels obligated to load the dishwasher, do the laundry, write a letter, and twenty other things before collapsing into bed. She giggled to herself wondering what men might want to learn from women.

Sifting through the mail Brenda found the mortgage and the electric bills, a magazine for Steve, and a plain white envelope. Inside the envelope she saw a flyer for a seminar at Coffee Encounter. A handwritten note read, *This could change your life.* She decided to save the flyer and deal with it in the morning. She stared at the ceiling wondering if she wanted to change her life.

Kristy:

Kristy walked out of Coffee Encounter and the humid air slapped her as if she had offended it. Sucking in a breath she checked her watch. She had a little time for window shopping.

She headed down 5th Ave toward the Plaza. Stopping short she caused the man behind to almost tumble on top of her. She barely heard his muffled curse because she was completely focused on the Saks window.

The dress was stunning in its simplicity. It had cap sleeves, a sweetheart neckline, tight bodice, and a skirt that would sway with every step. And it was the lightest lavender with black at the neckline and waist. For a second Kristy could actually hear it calling to her. But reality crashed in when the voice inside her head screamed, *You can't wear that! It would show every bulge. You're fat, remember?*

With a sigh she kept walking, head down until she got to the subway station. Her heavy steps made more noise than usual as she descended into the black hole of the green line entrance.

Once back home she walked to the kitchen and poured herself an orange juice adding a touch of vodka for flavor. Tomorrow would be better because she'd be at work and wouldn't have so much free time to wallow.

She thought about her job. Everyone was always screaming at her. Her boss, the customers, and the other customer service reps that claimed she took too long appeasing the customers. But Kristy didn't understand how they could rush to pick up the phone when the next person calling was only going to yell at them about a bill or a delivery delay. Why not just solve the problem so they didn't call back?

In order to have dinner on the table by six she had to turn on the oven now. It was just so hard to get up. She felt like a fifty pound weight was pressing on her chest. In the end the pain of getting off her schedule was enough to motivate her to rise and shuffle to the oven. Once vertical it was easier to keep the momentum for setting the table and preparing the meal.

Kristy was distracted bustling around the kitchen, chopping onions and peeling potatoes. The smell of the roast made her stomach growl. She peeked at the clock to make sure dinner would be done on time and saw the strange note on the white board. *Go to Coffee Encounter Wednesday at 6pm. It might save your life.*

What on earth could that mean? How could something at Coffee Encounter save her life? Oh well, Wednesday is Gary's bowling night and she's always looking for a reason to get out of the house. She'd go and find out.

Kristy heard the door open down the hall and called out, "Hi honey. Dinner's almost ready."

When Gary came to the table he asked, "Why are you staring into space like that?"

"Gary, did you write this weird message on the board?"

"Yes, when I went through the mail, there was a flyer for a meeting at that coffee shop you like. Someone wrote the part about it saving your life. I spilled my juice on it so I just wrote it on the board."

"Doesn't it strike you as strange?"

"Nah. I'm starving. When will dinner be ready?"

Snapping out of her reverie Kristy said, "Sorry hon, it'll be done in a moment." But inside she resolved to get to the bottom of this on Wednesday.

Joe:

Hours passed. People had come and gone. And still Joe sat sipping his tea. Occasionally he'd reach into his briefcase for a magazine or crossword puzzle. But mostly he watched the people strolling by.

He marveled at the couple outside. The way she gazed up at her man and laughed with her head thrown back. They must be in love. No one had ever laughed at Joe's jokes like that. It must feel incredible.

Noor approached and laid the paper, open to the want ad page, on the table in front of Joe. Then he smiled and walked away.

"What the hell are you implying, Noor?" Joe grumbled.

"I'm not implying anything."

"You want me out of your hair or something?"

"Joe, sometimes you just have to accept a gift when it's offered. Or people will stop offering." With that Noor went into the back room and shut the door.

Joe looked down at the paper but didn't pick it up. He didn't want another job. He wanted his old job back. He couldn't comprehend why they let him go. He knew mortgages like the back of his hand.

He went in to the office each day at the same time, ate lunch at the same place. He was comfortable there. At 47 years old he didn't know if he could start again.

His mom had always told him to step outside his comfort zone. She would say, "Joey, sometimes life isn't what you think it should be. You need to learn to let go and smell the coffee." He could smell the coffee here at Coffee Encounter, but he still wanted his old job back.

When Joe looked up he saw Noor standing beside him. With tea in hand Noor said, "Sometimes you need to look outside yourself to really find out who you are."

"You talk in riddles, Noor. I don't understand," Joe replied.

Noor shrugged at Joe like he wanted to say more. Then he went back to the counter to wash the mugs.

Joe picked up the paper and read the ads. Medical assistant- no. Housekeeper- not by the looks of my apartment. Office manager- no experience. When Joe turned the page a flyer fell out for a seminar right here at Coffee Encounter. On the bottom it read, *You really need to hear this*. He went to the counter to ask Noor about the seminar, but Stacy was there instead.

"Stacy, where did Noor go?"

"He left."

"But he was here a second ago."

"Well, he's gone now."

It was time to go. Joe was about to throw the paper away but something made him take the flyer out, fold it and put it in his briefcase.

Edward:

Edward picked up his messages. When he heard Erin's voice, a huge smile broke out on his face. He never thought she would call but he was glad she did.

Moments later, the delight of anticipation was replaced by the fear of reality. Edward was a flirt, who talked a big game, but he'd never followed through on meeting another woman behind his wife's back.

He sat down and gave himself a pep talk, "Okay man. It's not like I'd be having an affair. I'll meet Erin for a drink. Nothing wrong with two friends getting together for a drink." And he picked up the phone and dialed Erin's number.

"Goldstein and Smith, Erin speaking, how may I help you?"

"Hi Erin. It's Edward from the coffee shop."

Silence.

"Erin? Are you there?"

Clearing her throat, "Um. Hello."

"Is this a good time?" Edward asked.

"Yes, it's fine. I'm sorry. I'm just surprised you called. Actually, I'm surprised I called you first," Erin giggled in discomfort.

"I understand. But I'm really glad you did." Edward continued before he lost her to nerves, "Would you like to grab a drink after work?"

Silence.

Erin thought about what Ms. Goldstein had said to her earlier. Then she remembered that Paul was out of town on business tonight. Her heart felt like it would burst right out of her chest.

In a shaky voice Erin responded as Edward exhaled, "I can't usually go out for a drink but tonight might work…" Her words trailed off and she held her breath.

"Great! Want me to come to your office or meet at Silvio's? It's right across the street from Coffee Encounter."

A little too quickly Erin said, "No, don't come here. I'll meet you at Silvio's."

"Sounds great! Six o'clock?"

"That'll work. I'll see you there at six."

"Okay. I look forward to it. Bye!"

"Bye."

Edward hung up the phone. He dropped to the floor and did twenty pushups then jumped up like Rocky ready to take on Apollo Creed.

Sherri walked in and said, "Oh, I'm sorry. I didn't mean to interrupt you."

Edward put her at ease, "Don't worry Sherri. I was just finishing. But let's get everything in order. I have to be done by 5:30."

"If you have a meeting, it's not in your book sir. Do you need me?"

"Ah. No, no. That's fine. I'll take care of it. You can make it an early night."

"Thank you. Here's the number for the painter you asked me about earlier. I'll pull up the power point while you call." Sherri got started as Edward dialed the phone.

Erin:

Erin placed the receiver down with a calm, quiet air that belied the intense contradiction of emotions overwhelming her. She did the only thing a woman in this situation could do…she called her best friend.

Please pick up. Please pick up. Please pick up.

"Hello?" said Jan.

"Hey Jan. It's me, Erin."

"Oh baby! How are you? What's going on?"

"Jan, I don't know what to do. No one else would understand. I'm a complete mess!"

"Oh honey. It's okay. I'm here for you no matter what. I'm getting a glass of wine and I'll just listen."

Laughing Erin said, "It's only 2pm!"

"I know but what are friends for…I'm ready. Go!"

"Here's the deal. Things with Paul are a little, well, you know Paul. This isn't really about him. I met this other guy." Erin stopped and waited.

"Other guy? Hmm. What's he like?"

"He's ridiculously gorgeous. But more than that…he seems intense and confident. He makes me a little crazy."

"He makes you crazy?"

"You know that jumping out of your skin kind of crazy that makes you do things you shouldn't do? I know I shouldn't have called him.

Paul will kill me if he finds out. I should never talk to him again. It's…insane!"

"Wait a minute! YOU called him? Wow."

Erin finally calmed down enough to ask, "What should I do?"

Jan said, "Erin, I love you. I only want the best for you. I don't know this other guy from a hole in the wall but I've never liked how Paul treats you. I think you're the best. Follow your heart. You deserve to be happy. It's good for you to experience life. To get out there and learn who you really are. If you get scared, or need me for anything, you can get in your car and come straight here. I'll always be there for you, no matter what."

"You're the best, Jan! I don't know why but I think this could be good for me. I'll call you and fill you in. Thank you for everything. Give the kids a hug from Auntie Erin."

"I will. Hang in there honey. Everything is going to be all right."

"Bye Jan. Hugs."

Brenda:

"Mommy, Mommy, Mommy!" Sophie was three inches from Brenda's face and screaming at a volume and pitch that would make a beagle hide his head under a pillow.

Brenda sat straight up, "Sophie, honey, what's the matter?"

"Knock, Knock."

"What?"

"It's a joke, Mommy. Come on. Knock, knock."

"Sophie, it's 6:15 in the morning!"

"Mooommmmy! Knock, knock!"

Resigned to the inevitable, "Whose there?"

"Abby."

"Abby who?"

"Abby birthday to you!" Sophie fell on the bed in a fit of giggles.

Brenda couldn't help but grin. Ian and Zach would be up soon anyway so she pulled herself to her feet, put on her robe and threw Sophie over her shoulder. More giggles.

There was a note on the table from Steven. He had to leave early for a meeting. The heart he drew on the bottom made her grin. He was a good guy. Her automatic coffee maker started making noises and she envisioned herself having that first sip of coffee on the couch while reading the newspaper…POP. The vision faded when she heard Zach's whimper. And so it began.

By 10am the house was destroyed and Brenda was a wreck. Sophie was crying because Ian took her toy. Ian was crying because Sophie yelled at him. Zach was crying because he hated to miss out on anything. Dishes were in the sink, toys were covering every square inch of walking space, the coffee she never had the chance to drink was now cold, she was still in her robe and the doorbell was ringing.

Seriously?? she thought.

When Brenda peeked out the window and saw the cable truck it all came flooding back. She'd been anticipating this appointment for a week because it meant they'd be able to get both the Disney Channel and a faster internet connection, a win, win in her book. Looking around the room she briefly entertained the idea of pretending they weren't home.

Realizing the loud crying would give her away, she opened the door. As fate would have it the most attractive cable guy that ever walked the planet was staring at her. At her…in her robe…with her hair a mess… and a 'did I brush my teeth' look of horror on her face.

The phone rang so she pointed the hot cable guy in the direction of the TV and ran to answer it.

Steve said, "Hi honey. How's your day?"

"Oh, the usual," Brenda said. "Cable guy is here so I'll call you back, okay?"

"No problem. Love you."

"Love you." Brenda hung up the phone, took a deep breath, and dove back into her day.

Erin/Edward:

Ambivalent, Erin stood across the street from Silvio's. Her body defied every ounce of logic she possessed as it placed one foot in front of the other, crossed the street, and opened the door. Pausing in the doorway she almost turned to go when Edward strolled up to her.

"Hello Erin. The unmistakable fight or flight look on your face is scaring me," he teased.

Edward's good hearted joke calmed Erin's racing heart and they entered the restaurant together.

To the hostess he said, "Table for two, please."

Settled into what seemed to be the most romantic table at the most romantic restaurant she had ever entered all Erin could say was, "I like candles."

They looked at each for a quiet moment and the nervousness melted away. Edward ordered a bottle of wine and asked Erin about her job. She told him about how Ms. Goldstein was frightening in her dedication to the company but also protective and concerned about her employees. She explained how much she enjoyed the research and even mentioned there was a rumor that Mr. Smith might be retiring. When Edward poured her a second glass of wine she looked shocked. "I can't believe I talked that long about me!"

"Don't stop. I find you fascinating." He said with the most endearing expression she had to bite back her nervous giggle.

"Please tell me something about you," Erin asked.

Over a flavorful bruschetta appetizer Edward regaled her with several workplace stories that sent her into fits of hysterics. Her attentive amusement filled him with warmth.

"My wife used to find my stories amusing as well," Edward said.

"Your wife? I didn't know you were married. You don't wear a wedding ring." Erin was surprised and confused.

"I guess I assumed you knew but that was silly."

"Why did you ask me out then? I don't understand."

"I have no idea. Something about you called out to me and things with my wife have not been good for some time. That sounds so lame when spoken aloud."

"I think I understand. I have no idea why I called you either but its like something is missing and you can help me find it. That's weird, isn't it?"

Edward looked at Erin with renewed respect. "The only weird part is that it feels as if you are inside of my brain…like you really do understand."

They continued talking easily until the food arrived.

Erin smelled the entrées before she saw them. Her first bite proved her nose right…the Chicken Marsala was divine. Erin moaned in pleasure as she savored each bite and the way she stared at Edward's lasagna made him put up his hands in mock fear. He was thrilled with her enthusiasm and offered her a taste. She closed her eyes as she ate off of his fork and the sight made his breathe quicken. Spontaneously he leaned over and kissed her.

Her eyes popped open and he appeared as surprised as she felt. But as he continued to gaze deeply into her beautiful green eyes he saw the fear seep away and desire replace it. She leaned forward, and with his eyes never leaving hers, he kissed her softly. As her lips responded, his kiss deepened until it took his breath away. With no sense of time or space, his tongue wanted nothing more than to explore. It took all of his resolve to pull back. Stopping less than an inch away from her lips, he sensed she was overwhelmed too. Finally able to inhale on his own, he leaned back against his chair and asked, "Are you all right?"

"Oh my," Erin wondered how to continue. "I can't. I don't. I'm…"

Edward jumped in, "I'm so sorry. I should never have done that. I'm not that kind of guy. The moment…something came over me…"

Erin touched her finger to Edward's lips and said. "It's okay. I'm not mad at you. I'm just a bit scared of how powerful that was. And I feel like a fool because you told me you were married about two seconds ago."

"I'm very sorry. I know what you mean though about how powerful that was…I'm not sure my doctor would like to see how high my heart rate is right now." Edward kidded. "How about we continue our amazing conversation and I'll promise to keep my lips over here if you promise to keep your lips over there? Deal?"

"Deal!" Erin exclaimed in relief.

They talked and teased their way through another bottle of wine, a tartufo, tiramisu, and two cappuccinos.

Surprising herself, Erin was comfortable enough to mention her domineering boyfriend Paul. Edward was understanding and compassionate so she told him about Paul's drinking. She expressed her concern that putting her down didn't seem to be enough of a power trip anymore. She worried he might get physical.

Swallowing the lump in his throat Edward tried not to let Erin know how much it hurt him to hear her story. He had watched his mom go through a similar situation and hearing Erin talk made his stomach turn and his face burn with rage.

Sensing his anger Erin put him at ease, "I'm fine, really. I'm used to him and his moods. I'm sorry I brought it up."

Edward's anger dissipated when he realized it might have scared Erin. He said, "I hope you don't think I'm angry with you. I'm not. I want you to be comfortable telling me your concerns…telling me anything."

"For some strange reason, I am. Thank you."

The waiter came to clear the dessert dishes, "Will there be anything else?"

Not wanting the night to end, Edward looked at Erin who reluctantly said, "I really have to go."

Edward paid the bill and walked Erin to the door. She had to go downtown and he was headed uptown. He didn't want to leave her that late at night but she insisted. They hailed the cab in silence. Erin climbed in and Edward held the door and leaned forward. "May I?"

"Please," Erin whispered.

Edward gave Erin the softest, lightest, sweetest kiss she'd ever known. Then he closed the door and placed his hand on the window. She touched her lips as if to blow him a kiss but her fingers never left her smiling mouth. The cab drove away.

Even if he never saw Erin again, Edward would not soon forget this night, that kiss, or that smile. He walked the 22 blocks back to his apartment.

Noor:

Closing up shop, Noor felt the long day deep in his bones. He hoped for a decent night's sleep. He didn't want anything to infect his mission.

Noor thought back to when he'd heard the news. He was a different person then…self involved and scared. Much like the majority of the people marching in the parade we call life.

But things were different now. Noor had been given a chance to leave something behind, something bigger than himself. He understood things that people twice his age couldn't comprehend. Many people saw his 31 year old body and didn't realize his condition provided him the learning curve of a lifetime. And he was grateful.

His epiphany prompted his insatiable quest for knowledge and understanding and with each class he took, each word he read, each lesson he learned, he appreciated how little he knew.

Noor rolled out his yoga mat in the middle of the empty coffee shop. He stretched his taut muscles until they yielded with his breath like his thoughts yielded with reason. The moments of quiet cleared his mind. Ideas that had been vying for attention ceased to struggle and they came to him each in their own perfect time. One hour and hundreds of relaxed muscles later he finished.

He rose, rolled up the mat, and sauntered over to the counter. Important things needed to get done. Dialing the phone he anticipated her reaction.

"Hello?" Her voice quivered with age.

"Hi, Aunt Rose. It's Noor."

"Oh, sweetie. I'm so happy to hear your voice." Her delight was obvious.

"How are you?"

"A little pain but I'm fine, sweetie. Is everything okay with you?"

"Aunt Rose, I just called to see how you were doing. I love to hear your voice and I wanted to tell you I'm here for you if you need anything."

Unsuccessfully choking back her tears, "Noor, you are so very special. You are the only one who checks in on me now. Weeks and weeks go by and I have to admit I get a little lonely. Your voice brightens my day and keeps me going."

"Well, guess what, Aunt Rose? It's more than my voice that's coming your way. I need to get some fresh veggies and the stand by you in New Jersey has the best zucchini I've ever tasted. I'll be heading out there this weekend. I'll come to visit you afterward and I'm warning you…I'll be bringing a big basket of the freshest veggies you've ever seen!"

"Oh no. You don't have to do that!"

"Aunt Rose…if you don't let me give you this tiny gift from my heart you'll hurt my feelings. Especially after all you've done for me."

"When you put it that way, it's hard to refuse…"

"Perfect! I'll come by Saturday afternoon. Get your cards ready. I'm feeling lucky."

Her laughter was that of a young woman. "I'll be ready mister! Bye sweetie."

"Goodbye my Rose. I do suppose. My heart will beat, when next we meet…if not a moment sooner."

"Oh you," Her giggles carried through the line right into his heart. He loved the way she found joy in the little things in life. Pleased with how happy he made her, he hung up the phone.

Noor made one last special cup of coffee, turned off the lights, locked up the Coffee Encounter, and walked down the street to his apartment. He waved at the lady who sells flowers. When he gave the coffee he had made to Dan the homeless man, he received a magnificent toothless smile.

Noor jumped out to warn a taxi off of an errant little tyke, who by the sounds of his mother's screech was named Joseph. The mother glared at Noor and yelled at poor Joseph when she finally caught up to him. Noor shook his head understanding that you can't help everyone.

He continued on his way.

chapter 3

Indecision

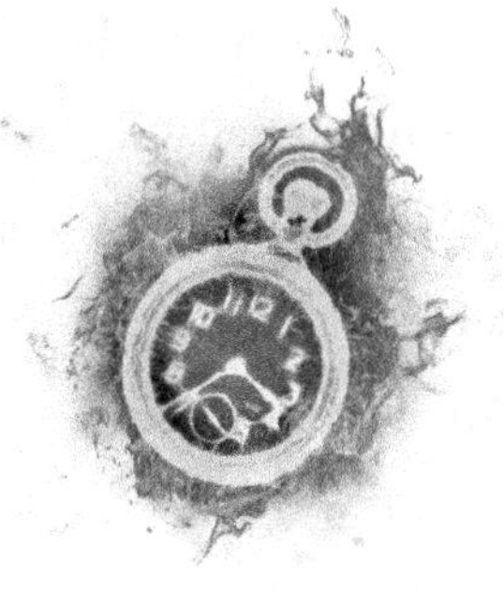

Noor was sipping his blueberry smoothie and writing in his journal when Joe arrived. He came up to Noor hoping for an explanation. "So, what is the big 'secret' about saving my life? What's wrong with my life?" As he said that last line even Joe realized how ridiculous it sounded. His life was a mess.

With a sympathetic smile, Noor replied, "I promise to answer that soon, Joe. Have a seat. Can I get you your usual?"

"Sure. Thanks."

Noor came around the counter and dropped Joe's cup. It shattered and tea spilled everywhere. "Good thing I have a mop handy. Don't get up. I don't want you to slip and fall."

"Hey Noor, don't you ever get riled up about anything? You're forever Mr. Calm, Cool, and Collected."

As Noor cleaned the mess he thought about what Joe said. "Gotta tell you, I wasn't always this way. I used to let things get under my skin but the anger wasn't serving me. I felt awful after losing control. Spent too much time apologizing and too much energy on worry and fear. It wasn't worth it to me so I made some changes. Breathing deeply doesn't hurt. Anyone can get there, Joe. Anyone at all."

Joe laughed heartily, "You know, Noor…that's the most you've said to me in the eight months I've been coming to Coffee Encounter!"

Noor laughed with kindness and headed behind the counter to throw away the coffee cup remnants.

Joe looked up when he heard the bell. Edward held the door open for Erin and she smiled and brushed past him. Joe recognized both though something was different about them. When he saw Edward hold a chair out for Erin, Joe sensed they were newly courting. He felt his anger boil, wondering how some guys get everything they want.

Thinking back to Noor's words, Joe took a deep breath. Like a sail with no wind, Joe's anger dissipated. He was still miffed but he guessed that had less to do with Edward and more to do with his nonexistent love life.

Kristy walked in and strolled over to the counter. "Hello Noor. It was so nice to get your invitation. Very mysterious and fun. Do you do these gatherings often?"

"Hi Kristy. Great to see you. No. This is a special event for a few special individuals."

"Really? How did I get on the list?"

"Because you're special."

"Oh my. Thank you. You know I don't think I'll have the caramel latte today. How about a coffee with skim milk?"

"You got it! Have a seat. Coffee's free today. I'll bring it over."

Kristy sat next to Joe and smiled a greeting.

Peering out the window Joe said, "I thought it was supposed to be beautiful today. It's starting to get dark out there."

"That's what I thought too, but I heard some thunder rumbling as I walked here."

Handing Kristy her coffee Noor looked excited. "It's getting darker. Sometimes the lights go out when there's a storm. What a great opportunity to light some candles. Want to help, Joe?"

"Uh sure," said Joe.

"I love candles!" Kristy gushed.

Erin responded, "Candlelight…how romantic," while Edward smiled.

With candles burning everywhere, Coffee Encounter glowed like a Christmas tree in December. Even Joe experienced a lighter and happier attitude with this new atmosphere.

Brenda bustled through the door. Shaking her wet hair like a puppy just sprayed with a hose, "It's starting to really come down out there! Am I late? I had to leave a list a mile long with the sitter."

Noor called out, "Not late at all Brenda. Have a seat and I'll bring your usual over to the table."

"Hey, nice mood. You should use candles more often," Brenda said as she sat next to Kristy and grinned. Kristy whispered, "Must be weird to be without the kids, huh?"

"It is weird! I was very excited about the time alone yet I keep turning around to see where they went."

"Hard to let that habit go. Whenever I hear a strange noise in the house my first reaction is to listen for the girls. And they don't live there anymore!"

Brenda smiled with affection. "I'm starting to appreciate you more and more. It's nice to see you here." Kristy was simultaneously grateful and embarrassed.

Noor handed Brenda her large mocha latte, no whipped cream, and she asked him who else was coming. To everyone's surprise he responded, "I think we're all here."

A loud crack of lightning exploded outside. Erin gasped and Edward put a calming hand on her shoulder.

"I hate loud noises," Erin murmured.

"What the…" Joe's comment was interrupted by another clap of lightning. The only light they had on flickered and went out.

"This is spooky!" Brenda giggled.

"Good idea about the candles," Kristy looked at Noor's expression and wondered if he had planned this. She shook her head thinking, *How silly! How could he plan a storm?*

"I shouldn't stay here in the storm. Paul will...be worried," Like a scared deer, Erin headed to the door. She stopped when Noor said, "Probably won't work."

"What do you mean?"

"Something with the electronic door gets weird when the electricity goes out. It's happened once before. You can try."

Erin's eyes never left Noor's as she tried to turn the handle. It wouldn't budge. The others could see the panic in her eyes.

Silence.

Then everyone started talking at once.

Noor picked up his cell and made a call. Then he sat down and waited. Kristy noticed and sat down. The rest followed suit. Edward asked the question spinning in everyone's mind, "Noor, what is going on?"

"First of all I called the electric company and they are working on getting the electricity up and running as soon as possible."

"Secondly, even if the door opened we couldn't leave right now. There are branches flying everywhere. It could be a small tornado."

The group looked at him expectantly so he continued, "I don't know what's happening either but I've come to trust that the universe provides. Sometimes when we are stuck, focusing on our own struggles, the world knocks and asks to be let in. Listening to the knock can provide the most opportunity to turn your life around."

"That's a load of crap," said Joe.

Kristy huffed, "Shut up Joe! Let him talk."

"Go Kristy," encouraged Brenda.

Noor continued, "Thanks. I usually wait and offer advice to people only when they ask. But you five have caught my eye. You all have such beautiful hearts….and yet there's a fine line each of you crosses into despair and selfish misery. Don't give me that look. Most people can enter the vortex of misery but you have the potential to not only improve your own lives but offer something of great value to the world. I invited you all here. But I can't make you choose the right path. The universe gives us a gift. But each of us has the choice of what to do with this gift."

When no one interrupted Noor smiled, "We're stuck here until the lights come back on anyway. Want to participate, have some fun, and maybe walk out of here with a new perspective?"

"I don't know," grumbled Joe. When the rest of the gang turned toward him he shrugged.

Noor explained that through his life experiences he learned the importance of living fully and contributing. He assured the group that he would give them more details as they continued but that in his intensive and eclectic studies he discovered the five most important aspects of transitioning from pain and discontent to joy and love and hoped to reveal them to the group.

He asked, "Before we begin does anyone have anything interesting to share with the group?"

Edward raised his hand. "No need to raise your hand, Edward. We can take turns and respect each other the way we want to receive respect, right?"

"Right!" said Kristy.

"Suck up," kidded Brenda. Kristy giggled.

Edward appeared ill at ease for the first time, "Something strange happened on the way to my appointment today. I was stopped at the light on 15th Street and looked over at the car next to me. A cute, young, blonde, probably in her twenties, was struggling to open a bag of chips. I know that doesn't sound strange but something about her stuck with me."

Joe chuckled, "I wonder what stuck with you. Was it the blond hair or was she also wearing a mini skirt?"

"Come on, Joe. It wasn't like that. It was just a feeling as she drove away. Then the light turned green and I forgot about her. A few miles later the traffic started to slow. There'd been an accident. I saw her car crushed like an accordion. I don't know who or what she hit but it was bad. I searched around and finally saw her. She was pacing, hysterical but alive. It made me think. You know? One minute you're opening a bag of chips and the next you could be breathing your last breath."

Noor waited to see if anyone would respond. When everyone remained thoughtful he said, "What happened there today was very powerful."

"I'm sorry Noor, but how is that powerful? It sounds just awful to me!" Kristy asked.

"That accident provided the young woman an opportunity to focus on the moment and appreciate life. But it also opened Edward to the concept of thinking beyond himself, the possibilities in change, and prepared him for this experience right now. It reinforces that I made the right choice bringing him into the group. Do you know how many other people saw that girl? The strange feeling you had Edward called out to you…and you had the good judgment to recognize it. You listened when the universe spoke to you. Great start!"

"You mean I heard a voice or something? I didn't hear a voice," Edward jumped in.

"No, when I say the universe spoke to you, I mean that the universe provides opportunities for you to learn. You have to be open to those opportunities to hear the message. Most people surround themselves with what I call the white noise of life…chaos and self absorbtion. In order to grow, people need to quiet the noise and simply observe and be."

"Hmm. That makes sense. I've had experiences like the one with the accident in the past but I ignored or downplayed it. I thought it was weird."

"Understandable," said Noor. "You were probably taught that intuition and perception were fluffy." Edward laughed. Noor continued, "And to focus on goals and achievements over the moment and the journey."

"Definitely. Talking about emotions was not my mother's strong suit and my dad wasn't around much." Edward recalled.

"The interesting part is that when you allow yourself to fully experience the moment you learn all you need to achieve your goals more efficiently and effectively." Noor gauged the reaction of the group. Primarily he saw nodding and expressions of interest with one exception. Joe was leaning back in his chair with his arms crossed and an expression of disbelief.

"Joe, tell me what you're experiencing right now."

"I don't know about this. How will this help me get my job back?"

"It must be hard dealing with such a huge transition in your life."

Joe exhaled, "Yeah. It's like the rug was pulled from under me. I can't wrap my head around it."

"It's fine to allow yourself a period of time for confusion and anger at the situation. The problem occurs when we stay there and don't deal with the transition. Don't answer now but for the next few minutes I'd like you to think about this…what positive consequence might come from this experience of losing your job?" Noor saw the look on Joe's face and added, "No judgment, Joe. Just think of a few possible scenarios. Humor me, man."

Noor turned from Joe, walked over to Erin and gave her a big hug. At first she pulled back in surprise then she melted into the hug as tears streamed down her cheek. "Why do you feel so trapped, Erin?" Noor whispered as he pulled out of the hug to see her eyes.

Sniffling she said, "I'm so confused. A part of me feels this intense need to get out of here and run back to Paul. He would be so angry to find I was here with you guys. But another part of me thinks being behind this locked door with the five of you is the safest I've ever been."

Edward reached for Erin's hand and said, "I won't let him hurt you again."

Noor countered, "Your intentions are good Edward, but you can't protect her. You're married and Erin needs to find her inner strength. Who knows what the future will bring for you both but right now the best thing you can do for her is to offer comfort and encouragement of the strong, resilient woman inside."

To Erin, "I don't know what happened to you in the past but your mirror seems to be cracked." Noor smiled to soften his observation. "What you see is not what everyone else sees. We look at you and see beauty, strength, intelligence, and the potential to give so much. You are whole and you don't need anyone else to stand tall."

"I don't know how I got here. I used to have dreams and hopes. Paul says…" Edward cut Erin off with, "Paul's an ass!"

"Edward, Paul needs your compassion." Noor interjected.

"What are you talking about Noor? Paul treats her like dirt and she deserves so much more."

"I agree that Erin deserves more. But think for a moment of the amount of hurt Paul must have experienced to be so insecure as to feel the need to constantly put someone else down. Erin would do well to find her way on her own. But passing blame without understanding the other person's situation doesn't help anyone."

"Are you kidding?" Edward raised his voice. "What kind of a man puts a woman down just to make himself feel better?"

"The kind that doesn't know any better. Paul needs help. But this isn't about Paul. It's about the six of us. Is your anger hurting Paul…or you?"

Between the truth of Noor's words and Erin's calming hand, Edward was able to relax his shoulders and breathe his anger away. "You're right. I'm sorry."

"Never a need to be sorry for wanting to protect those you care about."

Erin glanced at Edward. "I recognize what I should do but leaving Paul seems more frightening than staying."

Noor nodded, "Making the leap from the comfort of something painful to the idea of something better can seem like jumping out of a plane without a parachute. But you have a parachute. You have your own strength. You have friends who care about you. And you have the intellect to understand how much better your life could be."

"You could go back to school," offered Edward.

"I've always wanted to become a therapist," Erin faltered.

"Certainly would be a great way to give back. Others could benefit from your experience," Noor said.

Brenda added, "I could totally see you as a therapist, Erin."

The emotional roller coaster finally struck her and Erin collapsed into her chair with a sigh, "I need to process."

Noor turned back to Joe, "So, what positive aspect of your job loss did you come up with?"

"I don't know. The severance pay was a good thing," Joe struggled.

"Good!"

Brenda asked, "Noor, are we allowed to offer suggestions?"

"Of course."

"Losing this job could give you the opportunity to find something much better, Joe. A job with higher pay, less hours or maybe a career in a new, interesting field," Brenda said.

Kristy interjected, "Tell you the truth. When we spoke the other day it didn't seem like you even liked your old job that much. And isn't it nice to have a little freedom to do what you want while you're searching for something new?"

Joe cleared his throat and looked at the ground, "Um, I haven't really been job hunting and I definitely haven't been enjoying the time off."

Noor spoke up. "Isn't it interesting how someone from the outside can see things in a more positive light than when you are stuck in the middle of a problem? We can each learn to see things from a new perspective at any time though. You can skip ahead in your mind to possible results or a time when things work out. New solutions will come to you that you may never have dreamed up if you were focusing solely on the pain of the moment."

"I guess you're right." Joe pondered their comments, "But how do I figure out what to do next?"

Edward offered, "Want me to see if there are any openings at my company?"

"What do you do?"

"I'm a financial analyst, but there are always jobs in the marketing department."

"Hmm. Could be interesting."

Noor interrupted, "That's a generous offer, Edward. And Joe may decide to investigate it. But before jumping into anything, might I suggest a little introspection first?"

"What do you mean?" Joe asked.

"This could be the perfect opportunity to figure out your unique talent…to find a job you'd completely love. What are the things you most enjoy doing outside of work?"

"I like to read and looking up information on the internet. But how would that help me?"

"Those things can definitely be put to use in publishing, data analysis and a variety of other jobs. But keep thinking." Noor handed Joe a piece of paper and a pen. "Make a list. While you're at it, make two. One list of the things you're good at and one of the things you enjoy."

Joe furrowed his brow and tapped the pen on the table. This wasn't going to be easy.

Kristy offered, "I have an idea. Remembering how long you said you stayed with your old job, I'd bet you are loyal and dependable. Want to add that to the list?"

Joe looked at Kristy in surprise and said, "Thank you. You know you gave me a few ideas." He put his head down and scribbled away.

Noor turned to Kristy and said, "Tell me a little about how you see your life right now. Sometimes you seem frustrated and other times you're hopeful."

Kristy replied, "It's true. I find myself very confused these days. I've had a good life. But I feel…" Kristy paused and her eyes welled up with unfallen tears. She swallowed them back and continued, "I feel so discontent."

"By discontent, do you mean restless or blatantly unhappy?" Brenda asked as she gave Kristy's hand an encouraging squeeze.

"I'm not used to being this lost."

Noor sat down across from Kristy and said, "I don't have personal experience with this but many people I've spoken to put a lot of energy into their kids as they are growing up and, when they inevitably leave, struggle to find themselves. Is that part of it?"

"Definitely. Without that time consuming role of mom that I love there's just this emptiness. And my husband Gary doesn't…" Kristy struggled. "…see me."

"We will talk in depth about relationships soon but can you tell me more about you?" Noor asked.

"I'm a customer service rep. At times I like my job but most often it's frustrating. Every call is a complaint. By the end of the day I'm exhausted." Kristy spoke the next line so softly Noor had to lean forward to hear her. "And because I'm so tired I never work out. I'm heavier than I've ever been and I don't feel pretty anymore. It's not healthy but I find it difficult to get the energy up to do anything about it."

Brenda sighed, "I know what you mean about being too tired to take care of yourself. It seems like there are so many other things to do first."

"Let's turn this around for a minute." Noor suggested. "Do you think if you ate better and exercised daily you would be more tired or might it give you energy?"

"I don't know. I guess it could give me energy," Kristy answered.

Noor said, "Studies show that exercise and healthy eating is the primary way to increase your vitality and leads to a longer life. You need to find something you enjoy. Exercise doesn't have to mean going to the gym. Hiking, swimming, kayaking, running, choose an activity that you like. It will give you more energy and a positive focus to make you feel good inside and out."

Edward added, "That's right on the money. A hard workout makes me think clearer and feel less stressed. And Kristy, I hope you don't mind my saying, I think your smile is very pretty."

Kristy graced Edward with a huge smile and he said, "See!" They laughed.

Brenda offered, "Maybe we could find a class to take together. There's this dance class that combines zumba, jazz, and belly dancing. It sounds like so much fun. Would you want to do that?"

Noor added, "Working out with a friend increases the chances that you'll stick with it and is way more fun."

"I think that would be a blast! Not certain about belly dancing but I heard zumba is fun." Kristy replied.

"Don't discount belly dancing. I bet your husband would get a kick out of that. I know Steven would love it." Brenda laughed as Kristy grinned in embarrassment.

"So Joe, how're you doing with your lists?" Noor asked.

"Well, it was tough at first but once I started writing it got easier. Each new thing I came up with led me to explore another idea. Some of them are just plain silly though," Joe answered.

"That's great!" Noticing Joe's perplexed look, Noor elaborated, "You see if you never allow yourself the freedom to explore the ridiculous you never get to the original."

"That makes sense. Because if I hadn't added concocting crazy recipes under what I enjoy, I never would have remembered to add science to the list of things I'm good at."

"Do you see any patterns?" Noor asked.

"The top three that I enjoy are playing on the internet, making discoveries, and reading. The top three from my things I'm good at are cold calling, science, and organization. I'm not seeing how they tie together though."

"Hmm," Noor contemplated.

"Other than cold calling, I don't see a connection to being a mortgage broker." Edward added.

Noor said, "Good observation, Edward. Often people spend years at a job where they don't get the opportunity to use their unique talent. Taking the time to figure out how to use, not only the things at which you excel, but also the things you thoroughly enjoy, will help ensure you stay connected to the best path for you."

"Joe, your list has a ton of potential but don't rush to make sense of it yet. Sit with it for a while and maybe an idea will come that helps to illuminate your path."

Edward asked Noor, "As much as I'm enjoying this conversation, when do you suppose these lights will come on so we can feel less stuck?"

"Hmm. I believe the door staying closed is the only way to help you become unstuck. But I get why you're concerned. I'll make another call to the electric company while I get a tray of pastries from the back. I'm sure you're all getting hungry," Noor sympathized.

chapter 4

REALIZATION

Erin sensed a change in Edward, "What's the matter? You seem upset."

"It bothered me when Noor said I was married and that I shouldn't try to help you."

"But you are married."

"I know. But if I can help, why shouldn't I?"

"It pleases me that you want to help. You have already. Some of your strength must have seeped into me with the wine the other night. But I think what Noor meant is that before anyone else comes to my rescue I have to learn to trust myself."

Passing around the pastries, Noor chimed in, "Erin, you understood what I was trying to say perfectly. I'm sure you won't be alone. I believe though that you would feel stronger and more secure if you were with someone else because you wanted to be…not because you needed to be. It's empowering to know you can depend on yourself."

"You're right, Noor. I'm often uncomfortable when I'm alone. I bet it would be amazing to be relaxed in my own skin."

"I suspect that will happen for you sooner than you believe." Noor patted her on the shoulder.

"Edward, I'm sorry if I offended you man," said Noor. "This is a good time to talk about relationships and maybe we should start with you. Humans aren't meant to be isolated. We enjoy connection and our relationships alter whenever we grow and change. Sometimes the relationship grows with us and sometimes it doesn't. Do you want to talk about your family?"

"I don't know what to say. There are times when it seems like I'm wearing shoes that are a size too small when I'm with them." Chagrined Edward explained, "I love them. My son Brian is a cool, little guy. I enjoy hanging out with him now that he's old enough to play sports. When Elizabeth and I first got married we were that annoying couple that couldn't keep our hands off of each other and now..."

Noor explained, "All relationships go through ups and downs. It's not always easy to keep the romance when life gets in the way."

"No kidding! I don't remember the last time she reached for my hand or said *thanks for supporting us* or even *thanks for taking out the garbage*"

"When was the last time you said, *thanks for taking care of Brian and keeping the house in order*?" asked Noor.

Edward's expression was transparent. His wheels were turning.

"Someone has to go first," Noor continued.

"Huh. I hate to admit it but I don't thank her. I don't bring her flowers like I used to…I guess I was waiting for her to show me some appreciation." Edward seemed to sink deeper into his chair as he contemplated this new idea.

"I'll let you be with that for a minute, Edward. We'll come back to it." Noor turned to Brenda. "How is everything going with your relationships?"

Brenda answered, "You know, I think overall Steven and I are doing all right. He's a great guy and he's patient with me when I get all stressed out."

Noor nodded, "That's great. True love is when someone accepts and appreciates you for all of you …not just the good stuff. How are you handling the whole mom thing?"

"Being a parent is one of the great mysteries of the world. No one can make me angrier, more frustrated, and consider myself a failure as much as my kids." Brenda thought of something that made her face light up, "and no one can make me feel as perfect and loved."

"As you've found out, the relationship with your children is one of the most intense. You seem to have a much better understanding of life than the last time you were here," Noor observed.

"Yes and no. The other night I realized how much I love them and would do anything for them. But I still find the everyday acts of child rearing to be out of sync with my personality."

"It takes all types. The world would be very boring if everyone were the same. Some people are what we perceive as 'naturals' at parenting but it's just that…a perception. Everyone has flaws. And everyone has some remarkable traits to pass along."

Kristy added, "I was one of those naturals. Not that it was easy but I wanted it so badly, I put every ounce of energy I had into being the best possible parent. And guess what? I did my job well… and they still moved out. And now I'm lost."

Noor said, "It's all about balance. Staying true to who you are as a person keeps you strong and rejuvenated while understanding what an important job you have keeps you giving and compassionate. That's a fine line few people are able to master. And Kristy, you're not lost. You're searching."

Joe surprised Brenda when he finally spoke up, "You remind me a lot of my mom. She was strong. Sometimes she yelled but I never doubted that she loved me. And she always gave me the best advice. Too bad I never took any of it." They all laughed.

"Believe it or not, Joe, you warmed my heart!" Brenda went over and gave Joe a big bear hug. His shocked expression amused her greatly and she chuckled, "I need a potty break. Do you have a flashlight, Noor?"

"Sure." Noor handed her the light and she scurried down the hall as the rest of the group laughed.

Noor said, "So Edward, how are you holding up?"

"I haven't heard a word you guys have said for the last five minutes." Edward shook his head. "I've been contemplating if the spark died between my wife and me because we didn't take the time to fuel it."

"Probably," Noor was nothing if not honest. "But that doesn't mean its over. Realizing you two are both at fault is more than half the battle. Most people don't take responsibility when a relationship falters. They let the fire die, blame the other person, and walk out. Can you remember what attracted you to your wife in the beginning?"

Edward glanced at Erin and continued when he saw her encouraging expression. "Elizabeth was a ball of fire when I met her. She was fearless, had the most incredible laugh, and never backed down from a dare. Probably why she doesn't back down when she wants me to do something now," he reflected.

"You're right. Many times the aspects of people we most love in the beginning of a relationship can drive us the craziest after a time. Do you think it would be worth exploring a way to help her find her fire again?" Noor asked.

"Where would I start?"

Noor asked, "Any of you ladies have suggestions for Edward?"

Kristy stood up in her excitement, "What I would want is for you to come right over to me with a hug, a kiss, and a compliment as soon as you come home. It would show you miss her."

Catching the last bit of the conversation on her way back from the restroom Brenda added, "Make alone time for you two. Plan something special like a night out or a vacation or something. Even if it's simple, a woman loves when you put the thought into it without her having to spell it all out for you."

"Show her some respect. Listen when she speaks…see her, don't watch the game or read the paper as you listen. And if she has an idea or a dream don't ever tell her it's stupid or beyond her. Tell her she can do anything." Erin cleared her throat.

"You can do anything," Edward said to Erin.

"You're a fast learner!" Erin said.

"See, Edward. If you want to know how to treat a lady…ask a lady." Noor said.

"You ain't kidding, Noor! Thanks guys. But I have to admit I won't be telling Elizabeth my big change stemmed from the advice three women

I spent the evening with gave me…it might not have the same effect." Everyone laughed.

"Kristy, you had a great idea for Edward," said Noor. "Did you ever mention to your husband that you'd like him to pay you the same attention when he gets home from work?"

"Uh, no. Why do I have to tell him? Shouldn't he already know?"

"This is the biggest fallacy and cause of relationship challenge. We have to let go of the expectation that our mate can read our mind. If you want something ask for it."

"I never thought of it that way. I assumed that if he loved me he would understand. I wonder what he'd do if I told him I wanted more affection and compliments."

"Forgive me if this seems crass but I bet it would work if you implied the compliments would make you feel more desirable and may cause him to get lucky more often." Joe grinned when he realized she wasn't going to slug him.

"It's like in business…you have to put it in a way so that your clients understand what's in it for them," said Brenda.

Kristy thought about it. "I can do that."

"And what about friends?" Noor asked.

"What do you mean?" Kristy asked.

Noor clarified, "There can be a lot of pressure on a guy to feel that your happiness rests only with him. Do you hang out with your friends?"

"Gosh, I haven't gone out with the girls in a long time. I miss the fun we had talking for hours on end."

Brenda said, "I think women friends are even more important as you get older. If you want compliments no one is better than a girlfriend. And she's honest enough to tell you not to buy the hot pink mumu!"

"You crack me up, Brenda. I hope we can take that dance class together. We'd have girl time and I might lose a few pounds. There's no downside."

"I'd love to. I promise to get the information by next week."

The energy in the group had completely changed in the short time they'd been together. Each had come into the Coffee Encounter stressed and self-interested. In this moment of silence the feeling of camaraderie was palpable. No one was going to leave tonight the same person. They had each received unexpected friendship and insight that could change their lives.

"May I ask you something Noor?" Joe inquired.

"Of course."

"You seem wise well beyond your years. How did you get to be this way? At your age, you should be in full swing ego mode but you are here looking to help us. I want to ask what's in it for you but something tells me you honestly don't expect anything in return. It's throwing me."

Taking in a big breath Noor began, "I won't go into details because frankly it's not that important in the big picture. But I will tell you that I used to be very self-centered. I was headed in a downward spiral. One day I was thrown a life raft in the shape of genetic misfortune. My father died of a cerebral aneurysm. To put it simply, this means there's a weak spot in a blood vessel in your brain and if it ruptures you could die. He died very quickly which gives me solace that he wasn't in much pain. Cerebral aneurysms are sometimes genetic so they tested me. I found out I have one too."

Erin gasped. The rest of the group appeared shocked. Noor tried to appease them, "You can live with an aneurysm for many years. The healthy lifestyle I lead helps of course but you never know when it could happen. I wish I could help you to understand that this peculiar experience of mine was the best thing that ever happened to me. Before I found out I was frozen and useless…my life had a stranglehold on me that would have killed me slowly and painfully. Since my awakening I have turned my life around and dedicated myself to helping others. I know firsthand that life is too short not to live fully. I find choosing a small group of smart, passionate yet mildly misguided individuals, works best. This way I can pass along what I learned and they can then pay it forward."

Silence. Some in the group felt unworthy, some felt sad, a few wanted to scream out how unfair life was, while others contemplated the mystery of existence. But no one said a word. In their own way, in their own time, each understood that words were not necessary. Action was necessary. In some small way each person appreciated that the best way to repay Noor was to ingest the message and spread his wisdom.

"That's it!" Noor said.

"What?" Edward asked.

"I've been having these nightmares. I struggle with what they mean. Just now I realized I've been over thinking it. I don't believe my dreams are this deep dark secret. I have to get more information but I suspect this recurring nightmare is more of a recollection than a dream. I wonder if the person in my dream is my father and I blocked it. Excuse me a moment. I need to write down my thoughts on this to review later. Be back in a minute."

chapter 5

Escape to a Better Place

As they were waiting, the group discussed Noor's shocking revelation. Noor finished and returned with a satisfied glow and said, "I can't tell you how relieved I am. This has been haunting me for a long time. My father was very important to me and I don't want to forget or repress even a second of time with him. The painful moments are as significant as the joyful ones because they have led to turning my life around."

The light came on and the hum of the refrigerator was heard. Noor said, "I bet the door works now. You're free to go if you choose."

"What if we don't want to go just yet?" whispered Kristy.

Noor observed the group and said, "I suppose that's up to each of you. I did have two more steps to discuss."

With a sparkle in her eye Brenda stated, "If you'll also share your gift of how to make the all time best mocha latte, I'm in!"

Erin, Joe, and Edward all nodded and made themselves comfortable. Kristy requested, "Don't start until I go to the bathroom, Noor."

Joe said, "Oh yeah. Good idea. I'll go too."

"Take your time, guys. I'll get everyone another drink. Come on, Brenda. Don't tell but the secret is all in the chocolate." Noor waved her behind the counter.

Erin took Edward's hand, "I hope things work out for you and Elizabeth. Your son deserves the extra effort to make it work."

"Thank you, Erin. You're very special. I will be here for you…as a friend. Anything you need to help get you on your feet. Please tell me you won't stay in a relationship that is hurting you."

"I feel strong. I recognize that I should get out but his temper has gotten worse so gradually I put up with it…like the frog."

Edward gave her a puzzled expression so she explained, "If you put a frog in boiling water he'll jump right out. But if you put him in cool water and gradually warm it to boiling he'll stay in and eventually die. It's not that bad of course but I feel a little like the frog. I'm going to learn the lesson before I boil. The idea of going back to school is exciting. I bet my friend will let me stay with her until I find a place of my own. I will definitely need a roommate but I'm fine with that."

"You are so strong. You'll do whatever it takes. Any guy would be lucky to be with you. Probably won't be long before you find someone."

"I'm not worried about that. The idea of not being in a relationship is appealing to me right now."

Joe joined them and confessed, "You two made me mad when you first came in…looking all lovey dovey. But I finally realized I have to stop longing for what others have and get out there and grab what I want."

Edward responded, "If nothing else that was worth coming today, don't you think?"

"No doubt."

Kristy joined the group.

Joe leaned forward and softly said, "Guys, an idea is brewing. I'm not sure how but I have this urge to do something to help Noor. I have the time. And we can't just give up on him."

"Do you suppose he'd put up a fight?"

"Who'd put up a fight?" Noor asked.

Joe flinched, "Man, how can a guy carrying six mugs be so quiet?"

"Secretly, I'm a Jedi warrior," Noor kidded.

Brenda joined them and said, "Jedi warrior or magician. You even taught me to make a delicious latte!"

"Thank you. You're a natural, Brenda. Should I ask what all the whispering is about or should I pretend I didn't hear you?" asked Noor.

Joe laughed and said, "I promise to fill you in. I have to flesh out a few details in my head first. Will the suspense drive you crazy for a while longer?"

"Not at all. One thing I've learned is the importance of timing. Mind if I fill you all in on my fourth step while Joe deliberates?"

Everyone nodded so Noor continued, "Wishing you were in a different place seems like a waste of energy to me. The two options are to take action or to be glad in where you are. The reason I bring this up is not to say that hope is bad. It's to tell you how important action is if you want to make changes in your life. Many people are discontent, many people want to live more authentic and joyful lives, but only a select few do something about it. Does that make sense?"

Edward said, "I know exactly what you mean, Noor. I see it all the time in business. People talk about these great ideas they have but they don't do what needs to be done to make it happen. We call them the talkers and stop listening to them because we know they won't follow through."

"You're right, Edward. Many people talk about what they want and some people don't even verbalize it. They imagine what they want and come up with excuses why it won't work. You have the strength to take action. Before we talk about the steps to reaching your goals let's go back and check…have you gotten any clarity on what exactly it is you need to do to make your life better?"

Erin started, "I want to be stronger and more independent. I will call my friend Jan and see if I can stay with her while I get on my feet. Then I'd like to see what it would take to become a therapist."

"Erin, you're on the right track. You have some concrete steps you can take immediately and you are in touch with the emotions you want to acquire that accompany your goal. The desired emotional state is a strong motivator. How about you?" Noor asked Kristy.

"I don't have anything as specific or significant as Erin's."

"That's all right, Kristy. Talk out your ideas and we'll help you work through it."

"I want to get in better shape, reconnect with my friends, and spend more time doing fun activities with my husband." Kristy hesitated a moment then added, "…and I want to apply for the manager's position at my company."

"Wow, you never mentioned that. Tell us some more."

"I don't like being on the phones because everyone yells and there isn't anything I can do to help them. I want to be the type of manager that allows the reps to do whatever they can to help the customer and not just pacify them. Our managers' treat us like we're inadequate and I know the company would be better off with someone who empowers and praises the employees."

"You're a natural, Kristy. The company would benefit greatly from a dose of your positive spirit. Let me challenge you a little on the other goals you have. Consider making them more specific. For instance, instead of getting in better shape you could say that you want to work out three times a week, only eat sweets once a week, and lose five pounds."

"I need to lose way more than five pounds but I see what you're saying. Thank you Noor."

Edward said, "My goals right now are all personal ones. They don't seem very lofty."

Noor responded, "Balance is the key to success. You already have a career that you enjoy and you're active and healthy. The area that appears to need work is in your relationships. Focus on improving communication and family connection and it will help you in all you do."

"Noor, can I ask you a question?" Brenda asked. He nodded so she continued, "I feel extremely serene right now but I don't have any specific actions I'm thinking of taking. Did I miss something?"

"A wonderful yet subtle transformation took place for you Brenda. You have gained an air of gratitude. You have a husband that loves you, three healthy children, and the expectation of new business opportunities to come. A greater gift cannot be given than gratitude. The challenge for you will be to remember and practice it every day…especially during those high stress times that make you question yourself."

"Maybe that's why I feel so serene. For the first time in a long time I feel truly blessed. I've always been fortunate but didn't often take the time to appreciate it. Life is good."

"Yes. It is." Then Noor addressed Joe, "And you, my man, what have you discovered?"

Joe answered, "Based upon my lists and bearing in mind I would like a new career that I could get a kick out of, I'm considering web designer. How cool would that be? I have to tell you Noor I have this nagging voice inside of me that's dying to do something to help you out first."

A delighted Noor replied, "I'm happy to see how far you've come, Joe. As well as appreciative that I've stirred in you the need to give back. The final step I mentioned is all about that. Before we go there I was hoping to offer a few more tips for taking action because so many people falter at this point. Is that all right?"

"That would be great. I could use them." Joe replied.

Noor proceeded to tell the group about the steps he has found successful. He explained how important it is to define your goals with clarity. "Nebulous goals don't ever get achieved…or if they do you never realize it." Noor cracked himself up.

"Once you discern what you want to accomplish you can create a plan. Erin, you know what you want to do but there are many layers to it. If you don't lay out a plan it could be very challenging. Take the time to outline the steps such as: first, get an apartment, second, create a budget, third, apply for a master's degree, fourth, make connections with other therapists. You get the idea."

"Next step, prioritize. Kristy you have several goals you'd like to accomplish simultaneously. Certainly attainable but realistically, if you don't prioritize life can get in the way and keep you from your most important goals. You'll have to decide, but for example, I got the impression getting in shape is important to your state of mind. That will help you in all the other areas. When you create your plan prioritize your workouts as if they were business meetings or doctor's appointments. You are more likely to stick to them. By the way, I think that idea to apply for manager is a great goal to prioritize. You'd make a positive impact on the company and it would give you the confidence to realize all you are capable of accomplishing."

Noor was energized to the point of pacing by his next suggestion. He strode through the group talking about how imperative it is to take action every day. "Life is too short to put off taking action toward your dreams. Each of us deserves to live, love and give fully."

Laughing Edward said, "Man, you are like a pyromaniac because you really know how to light a fire under people. The way your eyes light up and the energy that comes from you, it's as if little sparks will come right out of the tips of your fingers!"

Amused Noor finally sat. "Can you tell I'm a little passionate about helping people find and follow their dreams?"

Brenda said, "Thank you so much for bringing us here, Noor. Everyone should get a dose of your wisdom. It should be viral."

"That's it!" Noor turned to Joe. "I got it. If you want to help me I can think of a way where you can help yourself at the same time. As you learn how to do web design you can practice by creating a website for me to pass this word around. My goal is to reach as many people as I can and get them fired up. Help them find what they are uniquely qualified to do then teach them how they can use their skills to serve the world. What do you think?"

"That's perfect. Your message needs to be heard. Too many people are living…" Joe struggled, "…like I was before I came here."

Kristy, "Noor, can you tell us a little more about this idea you keep bringing up about serving the world?"

"That's my last step, Kristy. And my most important," Noor said.

chapter 6

FIVE FRIENDS FIND MEANING

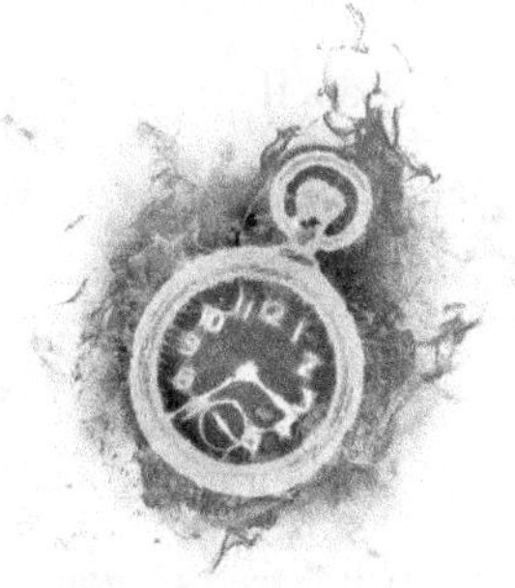

"Have any of you read the book or seen the movie Pay It Forward?" Noor saw a few nods and went on, "It's based on a concept of doing a favor for another person without expecting to be paid back. The only condition is that person then pays it forward by doing a favor for another...and so on. I have this idea of how to elaborate on this concept to fill both an internal and external need in each person. With me so far?"

He continued, "Too many people live a life of merely existing. Like zombies they do what they have to each day but don't get excited or passionate about anything. I believe that's because most aren't doing the one thing they are uniquely qualified to do...the special feature, talent, or gift they were created for."

Gathering energy from his idea Noor began pacing again and gesturing with his hands. "Just imagine how powerful it would be if each person used his or her unique talent to give back to others. The energy and passion being passed from person to person could eradicate the lethargy that has taken over. I might be a little over the top here but can you see how the idea of this could invigorate people?"

Standing Erin exclaimed, "I do. If I go back to school I could help inspire women to stand tall and believe in themselves. It's almost like I'm obligated to do it. It wouldn't be right not to. Know what I mean?" She blushed and sat down, uncomfortable with the excitement that came over her.

"Don't be embarrassed Erin. That's exactly what I was talking about… doing what you love to do, being true to you, then sharing that joy with others. It's the reason that I chose you five. You each have something to share."

"What do I have to share?" Kristy pondered.

"You have a light inside of you that's contagious. The plans you came up with today will help you rediscover who you are, what you enjoy, and will stimulate ideas for how you can communicate that light to others," Noor explained.

Seeing the confusion on Edward's face Noor said, "Sometimes the biggest gift we can give the world is through our children. Edward, you've already created a place for yourself in the business world. Now is the time to refocus on family. In doing that you'll find the balance that will help you move forward with the most success."

Edward gave Noor the thumbs up.

"In some ways the same advice applies to you, Brenda," Noor said. "Understanding how important your role as a parent is will help to make the mundane everyday tasks more manageable. And at some point in the future I see you putting that executive style into action. Keep a keen entrepreneurial eye open. I'm sure you will be able to find your balance with a home based business of some kind."

"I can't see myself not working, but the idea of going back to a sixty hour work week doesn't make sense. Having a home based business would give me the flexibility I need. But it's not following my dream if I start a business based solely on convenience, is it?"

"Part of creating a dream is building a balanced life. Some people recognize exactly what they want to do. Others know the life they want to live…flexibility, quality of life, time, and money to allow them to enjoy all of that…and then determine which options fitting those qualifications most interest them." Brenda's wheels were turning and Noor saw that the seed had been planted. He had no doubt she would find a career to revitalize her creativity while providing her children the attention they required. "When you find your dream be sure to give back and share it with the world."

Noor continued, "My grandfather was an inspiration to me. He used to tell me the best quotes to make his points. I remember one, I think it was by Plutarch but I'm not certain. It went something like this, "It is part of a good man to do great and noble deeds, though he risk everything." I believe in doing great and noble deeds and I see it more as a risk not to… because you're in danger of missing out on a better existence." Noor said.

"Don't wait until you are forced into reevaluation of what's important in life. Look inside right now and determine how you can take your life to the next level. When people attend your funeral…what do you want them to say about you? What impact do you want to make on the world? It's time to create your legacy."

BOOK 2 : THE LESSON

This book was written in two distinct parts because people learn in different ways. This will allow more people to find value and walk away with a renewed sense of purpose. In this section I wish to speak directly to you, to provide you with the stories, exercises, examples, and tools to find your unique gift. The concepts are the same as those used by the characters in the Coffee Encounter. But my hope is that you walk away, not just inspired, but with a plan on living the life you love and sharing your gifts with the world.

The observations and insights from the previous story were based on a five step process that has helped hundreds of clients take their lives to the next level. In this bonus section the five steps will be laid out and there will be tactics on how to use them in your life. They include:

5 Simple, Sensible Steps:

1. **F**reedom–helps you take back control of your life.
2. **I** am–helps you discover your authentic self, uncover blocks to success, better understand your strengths and challenges, and find your unique talent.
3. **R**eaching Out–explains how the changes you make to improve yourself will impact the people in your life. This step will provide tools for following your dreams while adapting more compassionate relationship strategies.
4. **E**xecute–shows you how to clearly define your goals, create a plan, prioritize, and take massive action.
5. **FIVE**–is the secret of how to use your newfound passion, talent, and skills not only to live a more joyful life but to contribute and serve others…coming full circle.

Each chapter will be broken down into what, who, how, when, and why sections for organizational ease. Here's what those sections mean:

1. **What**–explains the step.
2. **Who**–provides a personal story or a story of a client or interview that helps to illustrate how the step works in real life.
3. **How**–gives you hands-on exercises that you can use to make the step work for you.
4. **When**–shows which character from the first part of this book went through a similar situation and what he or she learned.

5. **Why**–clarifies why this step is important in your world.

How did these concepts come to be?

Discontent with the lack of purpose in my work, relationship challenges, and the constant fighting between my sons, my life was overwhelming. Ever since my fortieth birthday I had this indescribable dissatisfaction with every aspect of my life.

One day I visited with my friend Emma who wanted me to check out her new movement class.

In the hallway several women were chatting and laughing easily together. I introduced myself. They were all warm and open, but one woman stood out like a beacon. She was positively glowing. Her laughter was infectious and every comment from her mouth was uplifting and encouraging. As we went into the dance room I asked Emma about her.

"Oh, that's Judy. She's amazing. She's 61, has had cancer twice and lost her husband. She lives alone but has many friends and loves her life. She views every day as a blessing. Didn't I tell you the movement class I taught was for cancer survivors?"

Sometimes all it takes is a moment, one word, one thought to help you understand a concept with which you've been struggling. I knew something big had happened but I wasn't able to process it thoroughly until later. After seeing the class and experiencing the zest with which these amazing women viewed life I couldn't help but grasp the meaning of the phrase *life is what you make it.*

We are not tied to our circumstances. We get to choose how we respond to our situations. We can decide how to live our lives. Since then I've taken major steps to living a life I love. The lessons were so powerful for me I began to teach them to clients. There was an outpouring of gratitude and encouragement to take the message to a wider audience. You'll find that message here.

step 1

FREEDOM

What?

Many people go through their lives merely existing. They get up every day, kiss their spouses, go to work, come home, watch the game or read a book, go to bed…and do it all over again. And again. And again. Then as they approach middle age they look in the mirror and say, "Who the hell am I?"

They may vaguely recall the passions that used to keep them awake at night. They may or may not still love their significant other. They ask "have I become all I imagined?" Something is missing. They have lost their joy.

Want to *find the joy?*

Think about where you are right now in your career, health and relationships. Did you imagine yourself in a different place by this point in your life? Have you ever thought, "Is this all there is?"

Do you *want more?*

Has anyone ever told you "that will never work," "you can't make a living doing that," "you can't have everything you want," "Be more practical," or any other limiting statement? What happened inside of you as you heard these comments? For most it is like a fire extinguisher to the flame inside of them. Many people have been told "no" or "you can't do that"....and listen. Others learn to say "I don't care what you think. I'm going to do it anyway!"

Can you *take back control* of your life?

Often people go through life working, living, and fulfilling expectations that were set by others. Then one day, they stop and say, "I want more."

Is there a different path you wish you had pursued? A career you always thought would be fun? Do you have enough time or money to do the things you want to do? Do you have a connected, fulfilling relationship?

If you are at all discontent in your life and know there is something missing then STOP and recognize (are you ready for this?)...that you deserve to have all you desire.

Each person has a unique gift to share with the world. Somewhere along the path you may have been told you were lacking in some way and you may feel that you don't deserve to live a life you love, but I'm here to tell you…you DO. This is an abundant world in which we live and each person that exists authentically, fulfilling his or her destiny to give back and share their gifts, deserves the joy that comes with it.

If your energy is low and you are not excited about what you do, then you are not using your unique gift. You haven't yet found what you were made to do. When you use and share your distinctive talent your energy level will radiate.

Do you feel like your current life has been created or guided by someone else's views or beliefs? You wouldn't be alone. It's where the seed of discontent comes from…following someone else's plan.

You will learn how to do more, be better, and live fuller in the following pages. On the path to freedom, the first step is the desire to take back control of your own life and be true to yourself.

As you continue on this discovery constantly gage what make sense to you. Just as you no longer want to blindly follow the path someone else created for you, you will want to listen to your heart throughout this book and all future advice you receive. Be open to it all then process what works specifically for you. Release any preconceived notions and let your heart be your guide. The goal is to authentically live a life you love then share your gifts with others.

Who?

I used to close my eyes and imagine myself as a ball of Play-Doh. A big ball of Play-Doh with several colors squished together to make that indistinct lump that hardens if left out too long. I recall envisioning each person in my life that tried to mold me into who they wanted me to be. Several times a day, I would feel the life size rolling pin crush me flat. I would only lay there momentarily lifeless until another playmate would come along, pull me up and remold me.

One day I decided enough is enough. Instead of running from the inevitable rolling pin, I turned toward it, grabbed it, slammed it to the ground and screamed, "No More!" From this day forward I will be the sculptor of my destiny.

You have the power to become who you want. The power to go beyond existing and thrive. To make a difference in the world. To become your own sculptor.

Following the path that others created for you leaves you tired and dissatisfied. Taking back control of your life gives you strength and fulfillment.

How?
What makes your *heart race* when you think about it?

Finding the unique talent that will simultaneously bring you joy and serve others rarely comes solely from thinking it. You must also feel it. Is there a seed of an idea…a fond memory…or a dream of a future so big you can barely imagine it happening…

…that when you think of it your heart actually races?

Is there something that you want but have pushed aside because it seems too big or unattainable? Take a moment right now to sense where this idea leads. Your first reaction may be to push down the grand goals like running your own business, tripling your salary, or having the freedom to travel the world. This reaction is most likely a habit you acquired in your past that isn't serving you. Don't pass judgment yet on any thoughts that are stimulated during your reading. Be open and willing to explore.

For many, fear is all that is holding them back. Fear is normal. Everyone experiences it. Some let it stop them from accomplishing all they desire. Others use it, learn from it, adjust, overcome it, and achieve greatness.

I was petrified when I decided to go skydiving but I knew that if I could jump out of a plane at 14,000 feet, I could do anything. Any time I am afraid to ask for what I want, afraid to reach for a huge goal, afraid to be me, I think back to standing in the open door of the airplane and the exhilaration I experienced as I leaned forward and fell into being authentic.

Do you think that Harriet Tubman, Elie Wiesel, Martin Luther King, and Nelson Mandela didn't experience fear? No way. They felt the fear and took action anyway. Nothing great ever came easy. Working through obstacles and pain makes the achievement of your goal that much more real and powerful.

> **Exercise Alert!!** Now is the time to get a journal if you don't already have one. One journal in which you can keep and refer back to all of the exercises from his book. If you are going to do this…you might as well do it right, don't you agree?

Ask yourself—what resonates with who you want to be? Can you overcome your fear and be more authentic? For some that exciting idea that keeps them awake at night eludes them. It's all right not to know what your unique talent is yet. Discovering it can be half the fun. However, not knowing what dream to follow can lead to inactivity. The best way to move from stuck to inspiration is to take action. Try this exercise to get your creative juices flowing.

Get out your journal and make two lists. Don't filter out ideas based on internal judgments. Try to fill a page for each list.

List 1–Write down all of the things at which you excel (could be anything): math, golf, public speaking, good with animals, playing the piano, horseback riding, etc. If you are good at it…add it to the list.

List 2–Write down all of the things you enjoy: reading, playing video games, animals, flying kites, listening to music, carpentry, etc. If it makes you smile, jot it down.

Compare–Do you see anything on both of your lists? This is an area to explore further. In my example you'll see *good with animals* under List 1 and *animals* under List 2. Your first reaction may be "How will liking animals help me find my passion?" Don't judge yet. Sit with the idea as you move through the book. Any number of opportunities could come from this. New careers such as vet, park ranger, biologist, or trainer could be on the horizon. Or it might generate other insights and paths to contemplate. Keep an open mind and heart.

A Step Beyond–Make a third list of the gap. This is the area you feel needs more development or strengthening within yourself. It could be a quality such as determination or tolerance. Or it could be a skill such as follow through or financial proficiency. As you move forward it makes sense to reduce any gaps that could keep you from your goal. Once you recognize what they might be, finding mentors or resources will be easy.

"The more man meditates upon good thoughts, the better will be his world and the world at large." —CONFUCIUS

Bonus: Watch Your Words. Our words are powerful. The words we think dictate our attitude and actions. The words we speak infect not only our own actions but also those around us. Often people don't realize either the power or the control they have over their thoughts and speech. In order to take your life to the next level you must first recognize and control this significant road to success.

Don't concentrate on what you can't do….concentrate on possibilities. Stop complaints, blame, and excessive talk of illness and lack. If you focus on these areas they will increase. Anything you focus on expands. Create a new reality, a new habit, by stopping yourself when negativity creeps into your thoughts and words.

A friend of mine recently made great strides in this area. Every time she made a mistake she would say "Oh, what an idiot," "So stupid," or some other negative remark. One day I asked her if she would say that to me if I had made the same mistake. She was shocked. "Of course not!" she replied.

We discussed how important it was for her to give the same respect to her own mind and how powerful our words can be. Because her disapproving remarks had become a habit the reprogramming didn't happen overnight. She started by becoming conscious of the habit. Then she began stopping herself every time she said something unconstructive. The following week she was able to replace the negative thought with something more acceptable such as, I made a mistake. What can I learn from this?

It was challenging for her to add in more positive expressions like, I am perfect as I am, or I am strong and kind, but eventually she was able to make that leap as well. Within a few weeks she secured a new habit that included positive self talk. The shift this one change made for all aspects of her life was extraordinary. She was more confident and willing to take action. As a result she's recently landed a new job and a new relationship due to this one change in her thought process. It can be very powerful.

"The inner speech, your thoughts, can cause you to be rich or poor, loved or unloved, happy or unhappy, attractive or unattractive, powerful or weak." —RALPH CHARELL

When?

How does the concept of Freedom, of the realization you must be who you really are, occur in our story? Look back at Chapter 2. All of our characters go through the awakening to differing degrees but Erin is an obvious choice for demonstration.

Erin feels the discord with Paul and has become scared and embarrassed to have others see the way he treats her. The combination of her boss questioning her choice, her own discomfort, and her friend

Jan's support causes her to step outside of her usual decision process to explore what she really needs. At this point she is beginning to realize she deserves more.

Reaching out to Edward was the action that manifested from this internal struggle. The seed of self actualization that was planted for Erin in Chapter 2 continues to grow throughout the book.

Why?

You are an extraordinary person with a rare gift to offer the world. If you limit yourself you are actually depriving the world of the something special only you can bring to the table. It's okay if you don't yet know what your unique gift is- that will come. The first step is to acknowledge that if you are not living a joyful life, you probably haven't tapped into your distinctive talent yet. You deserve to be. And the world deserves what you have to offer. Follow your path and you will find an energy and abundance of love, success, and joy.

Begin by acknowledging that the goal may be to achieve success but that isn't what truly makes us happy…it's the ability to enjoy the entire process that brings true satisfaction. Enjoy this process.

An Aside:

Is your dream *changing*?

As people grow their dreams may change. Some who follow a dream still find themselves discontent. This can be disheartening if you follow this path simply because you believe it would be giving up if you didn't.

First acknowledge why you are discontent. Has your dream changed or are you going through a natural drop in the roller coaster ride of life? If you are on the right path but experience natural fluctuations in energy and success, work through it. Be determined and don't let anything stand in your way.

But if your vision of who and what you want to be is no longer the same, it's completely normal. Humans are not static. We are meant to change and grow.

As we create our successes, accomplish our goals, or simply grow and find new values and place emphasis and importance on other areas… our dreams may *change*. That's perfectly acceptable. Be flexible enough to go with it and adapt your aspirations to incorporate your new ideas and goals.

A Call to Action:

- Get a journal to keep all of your ideas/exercises.
- Create a new habit of success by stopping yourself when your thoughts or words limit you.
- Make and continue your lists of what you are good at and what you enjoy.
- Revel in the process!

step 2

I AM

What?

Before you can make any changes or act on the ideas you've discovered in Step 1, you will need to get to know yourself on a whole new level. Believe in yourself...in your faults, beauty, imperfections, desires, strengths, challenges, and gifts that are unique to you. Learn to trust all aspects of who you are.

Let go of guilt, self judgment, failure, and accept yourself with compassion. Quiet any voices that say you can't. Put aside your fear. All actions in the past come together to make you who you are today...a beautiful mosaic with unlimited potential.

Acknowledge that any emotion is valid and part of the process. The quality of your life is based on how much time you spend on each emotion. When you get upset or angry do you stay that way for weeks and take it out on everyone around you? Or do you get upset for a short while, let your frustrations out with a brisk run and move on? Your life will have very different results with each answer. Don't beat yourself up for negative emotions. Simply limit their shelf life in your head and find the strategies to learn from them.

Take a moment to consider the possibility that what you want **is** actually possible. Think about it. Visualize it happening. Imagine having the ideal relationship, the perfect job, every success. Often we want something fleetingly but don't believe the desire is within our reach. Sometimes getting what we want means leaving what we have…however uncomfortable.

"We must be willing to let go of the life we have planned, so as to accept the life that is waiting for us." —JOSEPH CAMPBELL

An Aside: Inspired to write, dance, call an old friend, drive to the beach, sing, skip, hug your child, or anything else that might bring you joy? If so, go for it. Don't pass those opportunities by that will bring a smile to your face and a beat in your heart.

Who?

When I was growing up my father hated his job. He worked hard and the upheaval of shift work made any kind of sleep schedule virtually impossible. He would walk in the door at the end of the day with head down, chest sunken, and a drawn look upon his face.

Unfortunately he never believed he could leave his job and pursue his dreams. He never even discussed what they might have been.

When he had time we hiked together. I remember once, while resting by the brook, he turned to me and said, "Heather you can do whatever you choose with your life. Please make sure you do something that makes you happy." His look was simultaneously wistful and urgent. I vowed to take his advice and never allow myself to feel like I was out of options. I never wanted to do something I absolutely hated. If you get creative enough there are ways to find the joy. To do what you love. Or at the very least- love what you do.

"I have not failed. I've just found 10,000 ways that won't work." —THOMAS EDISON

We often dwell on the mistakes we make or the challenging events that occur to block our way. If we change the way we think about those events we control our emotions, our outcomes, and our destiny. Stop judging. Revel in being human. Yes, we all make mistakes. But we can learn from them. We can grow and move beyond our circumstances.

For example, a coaching client of mine had trouble overcoming a painful relationship breakup from her past. (Yes, we've probably all had one, well, okay, more than one.) At the time of the breakup she was only able to see the darkness, the pain, the injustice of it all. But now, so many years later she can sincerely be thankful for the experience.

Getting out of the relationship opened many beautiful new paths for her. Going through the pain taught her to be strong. She wouldn't have been able to find the wonderful person she's with now if that other breakup hadn't happened. And she's come to the realization that she can love herself and doesn't need to depend on others for her validation.

Why wait years to get to that better place? It's possible to feel the gratitude in the moment. See the benefit now.

Make the learning curve smaller by visualizing yourself in the better place, with the growth and learning, right in the moment of pain. It eases the pain and provides a more open, wise place to be. Accelerate the process by visualizing where you will be or what you will learn from each experience.

If you have had challenges in the past, you can learn to find the good in the bad. Think of the lesson. How will the experience serve you down the road? Why wait to be grateful? Imagine how it will feel today.

How?

The process of self discovery is personal. Each individual may find a different tip or technique helpful. The following list gives you choices on ways to find your strengths and develop your passion. Use what works for you but come back to it again in the future. You may find a different suggestion helpful the next time.

As you make your way through this process remember to open your mind and not limit yourself or judge your answers. There will be plenty of time in the following steps to refine and focus. Right now it's about letting go of anything that may be hindering you and opening your heart to your endless possibilities.

1. Sit down with a few friends or family members that are close to you. Ask them to join you in this revealing exercise. Offer to give them an inventory of their traits or behaviors that stand out to

you then ask them to do the same for you. For example you might have someone tell you they see you as generous, kind, funny, dependable, but at times a worrier. It can be enlightening to learn how you are being perceived by others. The answers could guide you to a unique talent you never even knew you had.

2. Chomping at the bit to get started? Remember a long lost talent you'd like to pursue or a dream from your past that now seems within reach? Go take one action toward that goal right now. It can be something small. Make a call, get a book, go online and do some research, put together a list or a plan. The only way to know if it's a worthwhile pursuit is to take action.
3. If you are still familiarizing yourself with who you are, what you want, and what you need to know to get there, daily journal writing will help. Write every day even if it's only a few sentences. Begin by naming one or two things you are grateful for to get you in a positive, abundant state of mind. Then write. If you begin journaling about something that surprises you, don't question it. Just write because writing is a direct link to release the power of your subconscious mind. You will look back and use this tool later for idea searching. But in the beginning it is a way to release your creativity, make sense of your emotions, and work through challenges. If you have trouble coming up with anything at all use a starter phrase like "I wish…" or "If I could do anything…" After that the words will flow. (Note- date these journal entries. You'll find that helpful when you look back later)
4. Take a look at some of your core beliefs, your instant reactions or views on life. Did you acquire them from someone else or are they

all yours? Many people find they stand firmly behind something but can't quite verbalize why. Typically that's because it's a belief that was handed down but not formed internally. It's important to open yourself to new ideas or belief systems. Don't necessarily take them. Just be open to them and then make your own decisions. For most, creating a new habit of living authentically will take time and practice. However, it will be worth the effort.

5. Become a student of life. Discover more about what is available by reading books on success, looking through college course descriptions, watching and listening to people you admire. Always keep learning and growing. This one aspect of constant self improvement is something all of the most successful, satisfied people in the world have in common. Join their ranks and absorb like a sponge.
6. We are so often pulled in different directions we don't know who we are or what we want. It becomes imperative to make time each day to be quiet. If you meditate or do yoga that would be optimal. But if not, simply put aside a small portion of the day to sit quietly. Some people will find this more challenging than others. I admit to being one of those people. If you are as well, start small- just one minute a day. Once you get the hang of it you can extend the time. The benefits? Reductions in stress, clarity of mind, boost positive energy, and improve productivity. The habit of being quiet will help you get a clearer picture of how to live a more joyful life.
7. Learn to understand your temperament and style. Recognizing your strengths and how you view the world will accelerate the

process. Anyone can do anything they choose if the desire is great enough. However, if you can comprehend what parts of your style might be holding you back you will be able to change the way you view things and overcome challenges more effectively. To achieve greater success it is imperative you understand your behavioral style, your strengths, and the parts of your personality that you might want to adapt. Successful people understand how they respond to situations and how these responses will affect others. Learning to adapt behaviors in certain circumstances will improve relationships and place your goals within your grasp (You can learn more in greater depth by taking a behavioral profile. I use DiSC in my coaching but there are many options available).

8. Visualization of the life you desire is a powerful force that will contribute to achieving your goals. When you visualize what you want, make sure to be very clear and include all senses. Imagine achieving your every desire. Touch it, taste it, hear, smell, and see it…how will it feel to have it? Write it down in your journal. You will want to leave space to add pictures. Look at what you envisioned and feel the success every day. Make a small version, one picture or a vision statement to carry around with you. Whenever you reach in your pocket or purse and find it, it will remind you and the universe of your dream.

When?

An example from our story comes from Chapter 3. Throughout the book, Joe's tendencies lean toward stability and he doesn't like change.

Like many people, Joe was so resistant to change he was willing to remain in pain to avoid it. That doesn't mean people with his temperament can't change. It means they are less comfortable with it. Once they come to terms with that aspect of their personality they will better understand that their hesitations to moving forward might stem from this discomfort and not from any necessary risk.

Noor gets Joe to realize how important it is to adapt to the changes that are bound to happen in life. Joe was stuck focusing on loss until he adjusted his viewpoints on change and transition. He came to realize there are opportunities in every challenge.

Joe learned to become more comfortable and future-oriented during times of change. This adjustment enabled him to make it to Full Circle, the 5th step in our process. More to come on that.

Kristy was in conflict because her temperament was one that desired to relate to people but her kids' leaving and lack of unity with her husband was creating loneliness. She discovered that she had been concentrating on her roles and not on knowing herself as a whole person.

Her realization helped her refocus on finding ways to connect with her own goals, such as her desire to move into a management position, living a healthier life, and socialize more with her friends.

Why?

Are you where you thought you would be at this point in your life? Have you accomplished all you imagined you would? Is your music written, your dance performed, your dream fulfilled? If your answer is no, remember that life is short.

Life happens. Time passes. And the only reality is this moment in time. We don't have forever. Regret is an emotion that many experience but few would choose. Live your life to the fullest. Make an impact. Be authentic. Accept yourself and others fully.

Don't wait until you are forced into reevaluation of what's important in life. Look inside right now and determine how you can take your life to the next level. When people attend your funeral…what do you want them to say about you? What impact do you want to make on the world? It's time to create your legacy. Decide and take action. No regrets.

A Call to Action:

- Quiet your mind for a period of time each day and your authentic voice will guide you in finding your unique talent.
- Learn something new every day. Read, explore, ask questions, and discover what has worked for others.
- Clarify and add energy to your goals with vivid visualizations.
- Practice gratitude!

step 3

Reaching Out

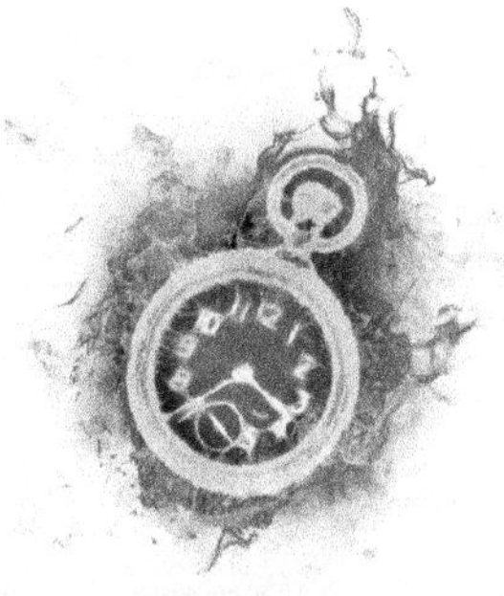

What?

The many relationships throughout our lives have shaped who we are and perhaps even who we want to be. There is an interesting dichotomy with relationships. Taking chances and letting people inside your heart is the only way to live fully. And yet you are the only person you have to be with for your whole life. You must be true to yourself. If you can learn to accept yourself as you are then you will be able to accept others for who they are. Practicing acceptance and compassion for self and others is a valuable life lesson.

Look inside and know who you really want to be. Then surround yourself with like-minded people and you will have the capacity to take your life to higher levels of success and joy than you ever imagined.

Who? AND How?

For this section, the stories and the exercises are combined for clarity of the message and an easy way for you to choose which relationship sections relate specifically to you. There are many different types of connections. No matter what your current focus the ability to improve your communication skills in general will serve you.

Significant other:

Being in a positive, loving relationship has numerous benefits both physically and psychologically. Of course that also means that if you are in a restrictive, negative, or unhappy relationship it's time to take a closer look at what you want. Change may be in order.

It's important to start with the significant other because this is the relationship that could most easily become strained during your self-discovery journey. Significant other sounds detached and cold. But with so many different variables it seems to be the best option in categorizing the relationships we have with those we love as partners in our journey through life.

When one person changes and grows, it often creates tension and fear in those close to them…even if the change is constructive. This dynamic can lead to stress or even an end to the relationship. But it doesn't have to. Love deserves every opportunity to grow along with you.

If you are the one that wants to change and grow and follow your dreams, recognize that your loved ones might inadvertently attempt to hold you back. Not to intentionally harm you, but because they are fearful that you will be hurt, experience failure, or your growth could take you away from them. It can be disconcerting when the partner you thought was in alignment with you, can't accept change.

When you appreciate their pure intentions, you are more able to come from a place of compassion when dealing with them.

However, being compassionate of their emotions doesn't mean giving up your goals. Don't allow your dreams to be pushed aside to preserve the relationship. This is not the only option. A solution can be found that works for everyone.

Achieving a balance with your relationships is important. First and foremost, know who you are and what you desire. People who love you will want you to be happy.

Deal with any unsupportive feedback by letting them know you need their encouragement and acceptance.

One of the primary blocks during this time of transition is that your significant other may feel distanced from you. Allow your family and friends to experience your joy.

Some people will appreciate talking for hours about your hopes and dreams. Others will just want an overview. And others may simply want to see your happiness.

Share your hopes and dreams. Don't expect a certain response but know that giving of yourself in this way is moving and will serve you and your partner better than letting your feelings go unsaid. That would create regret. And regret is a useless emotion.

The best way to gain insight as to where your partner is coming from is to ask them. They may share ways for you to adapt your behavior to develop the relationship. For example, you might be the type of person that wants to connect with your significant other as soon as they walk in the door while they may need time to decompress from the day. Discussing the differing needs, and giving that person the time they require when they first come home, is an easy way to make them happy and more inclined to focus on you and your needs.

If you have tried to adapt to improve communication…tried to share your dreams and joy…tried to connect, and you still are being met with negativity and oppression it is time to reevaluate the relationship.

Children:

There are many different roles in life, and without a doubt parenting is among the most challenging. That is why it is also among the most rewarding.

When you make the decision to transition to a more joyful life it will affect your children. Any change in their routine or what they are accustomed to can cause pandemonium. But think of the lesson you will be teaching them! A lesson so few people witness first hand…the importance of following dreams, never giving up, and taking action to accomplish a goal that will bring joy to themselves and others.

Many of us try to be the perfect parent, doing everything ourselves. We play games, read stories, bake cookies, and take them to every play date and music class. We use flashcards and create interesting imagination games.

We try to do it all and even turn down friends or family who offer assistance. Stores sell Supermom and Superdad shirts for a reason. But an ongoing drive to do it all will cause stress and isn't in the best interest of the child.

Before you get to the point where you start to lose it, think instead of the phrase "it takes a village to raise a child." If you have multiple children you can't possible do it all and give each child the attention he or she craves. The stress can make you impatient. The superparent mentality doesn't serve anyone.

Asking for help gives someone else the pleasure of giving, allows you the opportunity to reciprocate, rejuvenates you so you are better for the kids and yourself, and gives the children a chance to be open to and learn from other people. Ask for help. This is an important concept as you work toward new goals so I'll repeat it. Ask for help.

A technique I've found useful if you have kids and plan on starting a business from home, going to school, or researching new opportunities, is to focus on them first. To avoid the "who can get mommy's attention by screaming the loudest" game spend a little time giving your undivided attention to them. Then they'll be more inclined to come to your aid when you most need it. Set clear expectations then follow through. A new habit of cooperation will ensue.

There can be negative, albeit amusing, aspects of following your dreams while childrearing. Here's one of the payoffs. Your kids are the all time best teachers on joyful living. Just because they're small doesn't mean they don't have some very valuable lessons to impart.

If you want to learn how to experience true joy…watch a child. They are able to squeeze every precious moment from life. Children can look at a box and see a race car, a rocket, a fort, or a sci-fi transporter. A knock, knock joke can lead to fits of uncontrollable laughter. Cloud formations can be science, fantasy, and meditation all rolled into one.

Watch a child and see how he absorbs and appreciates everything right while it's happening. He isn't thinking of something that happened yesterday or something that may happen tomorrow. He is completely focused on the moment. And that is why he exudes such joy.

You can practice this same concept. Don't think back with guilt about something you did or didn't say or do. Don't worry about the numerous challenges that will probably never come anyway. Simply be in the moment…completely.

One of the best things I learned from parenting was that in order to teach compassion you have to be compassionate. If you want to teach love, you have to be loving. If you want them to respect you, you have to be respectful.

One day I found myself so frustrated with my oldest that I yelled, "Why can't you just be kind and nice!" When he replied, "Well mommy, yelling isn't kind and nice either," it hit me that we must demonstrate the lesson to be most effective. It's no longer a "Do as I say, not as I do" world.

The best thing I did was to tell my sons "I love you" when they were being unlovable. Everyone desires unconditional love. And that is what will heal and teach most successfully.

This one lesson can be very powerful whether you have children or not. Apply it to yourself when you are going through the process. When you make mistakes, are having a tough time, or simply feel alone, remember…unconditional love and acceptance. We all deserve it.

Family you grew up with:

Family fascinates me. The support we can give and receive from family is unmatched. And yet…have you ever met a person that didn't have a major complaint about a family member?

The idea that they will always be there for you can be the cause of both the pain and the pleasure. Family is the foundation of who you are, and with most families they will be there for you when others won't. On the other hand, if they are negative personalities, it is exceptionally difficult to simply remove them from your life. I have a wonderful family that with no doubt in my mind would do anything for me. And yet we all often kid there are a limited number of days we can spend together without ending up in a brawl.

Remember that any discouragement you may have received from your family was probably done with the best of intentions based upon your family's own belief system.

As you work through the next section of exactly how to acquire the life of your dreams you may be inclined to think "but so-and-so told me I couldn't do that!" Please remember with compassion that person was most likely looking out for you. Then remember not to listen to a word of it!

Friends:

"At times our own light goes out and is rekindled by a spark from another person. Each of us has cause to think with deep gratitude of those who have lighted the flame within us." —ALBERT SCHWEITZER

Several times in my life I have struggled with transition…changing careers, relationships, raising a family, starting a business, and reinventing myself. I have found that when I was going through my toughest transitions people came into my life with help and direction. Some for a very short time and others will remain close forever. The lessons weren't always obvious. If my eyes or heart were closed I would have missed them.

One example was meeting numerous women in a very short time that had successfully navigated challenges similar to mine. It was comparable to when you think of buying a car and then see that model everywhere on the road. When you focus intently and put energy toward a particular thought, solutions appear.

One woman I met that year was a recreational director at a resort. She was our guide in this beautiful, intermediate level hike. It was a tough climb but we still managed to chat. The more she talked the more we connected. A few years prior she had gone through marital difficulties, parenting challenges, and occupational restlessness. And yet her positive outlook was encouraging.

When she decided to leave her position in her ex husband's company, she made a list of all the things she loved doing. It included hiking, skiing, swimming, and golf. Many people would look at a list like that and think "I can't get a job doing these things. I'll just find something, anything, to make money." She didn't do that. Instead she hunted down a job that included doing everything on her list...that of a recreational director at a resort. Sometimes you just have to get creative.

Many people believe friends are important when you're young. Friends become even more important as you get older. The wonderful thing about friends is that you get to choose them. You don't have to continue to interact with someone that is negative, unsupportive, or following a different path. You have the choice.

Surround yourself with people who lift you up and make you laugh. Life's too short to continually listen to people who complain. If you are on a path to improve your life begin by consciously choosing to be with positive, energetic, and joyful individuals.

Workplace relations:

Unless you are the boss, the likelihood you can choose everyone you work with is slim to none. It then becomes much more essential to learn how to adapt to different types of people.

Your boss may be a dominant style that values action and results. If you chat by the water cooler and crack jokes at the meetings your longevity in that position might be in question. Even if you are the life of the party in your other roles, you need to adapt your behavior around your boss to be more direct and focused. He or she will appreciate the efforts.

Recently, I was consulting for a manufacturing company on improving communication and inspiring the staff to be more productive and effective. I uncovered an interesting dynamic.

The people in the customer service department were hired primarily because of their upbeat, friendly nature and ability to ease the concerns of the clients to create customer satisfaction and loyalty. Smart hiring decision.

The people in the production department were hired primarily due to their impeccable attention to detail and quality control. Also a smart choice.

But do you think the two departments were communicating effectively? Not at all. The customer service department would provide production with long winded instructions and unorganized forms. Production would cut off the pleasantries and demand what they needed. Customer service found the people in production rude. Production found the people in customer service lazy. Neither were appreciating the positive aspects of their attributes or adapting their behavior to improve communication.

They needed to learn to communicate better and ultimately to become more productive as an organization. During a group brainstorming session, people from each department expressed how they were being impacted and how better to communicate and operate with the customer in mind.

From these discussions, people in customer service learned to spend more time and attention to detail when submitting orders. It made sense to them once they understood how important it was in the overall value to the customer.

Employees in the production department learned the value of customer relations and interacted in a more congenial way for better internal service and teamwork. Their clients benefitted with improved service and the increased profitability pleased management.

This concept of understanding style and temperament is even more imperative if you own a small business. Often entrepreneurs hire employees that are like them because they feel most comfortable around those people. That isn't always the best option when you have a small company. Hiring someone that has a different skill set often makes more business sense. You want someone to be able to do the things you either aren't good at or don't want to do. No small business needs too many chefs and not enough bottle washers.

You can make changes to cooperate in your workplace by taking the time to understand the needs of the other person. Focus on the positive, give others the benefit of the doubt and then adapt your behavior to relate most successfully.

When?

In chapter 4, Edward learns a precious lesson about valuing relationships. As with many couples Edward and his wife Elizabeth had lost the fire and were living like roommates, rather than spouses. Each had forgotten to show appreciation and love and was more focused on their own needs than on what they should be doing to cultivate the relationship. Recollecting what attracted Elizabeth to him in the beginning helped Edward understand what he would lose with poor choices.

Edward knew his son Brian was feeling left out and desperately needed attention. Never meaning to hurt his son, work had simply gotten in the way. The whole family will benefit from Edward's ability to change his mindset and concentrate his attention back on the family.

Why?

When you are around people that are younger than you, you typically feel young and energized. When you are around people that are motivated and focused, you become inspired to do your best. When you are around people that smile, laugh, and enjoy the moment, you are more inclined to see the beauty in life. Create an environment of success by surrounding yourself with amazing individuals.

As you travel your road to success keep in mind the important role relationships play. Being able to satisfactorily navigate all of your associations will increase your chances to achieve a balanced, joyful life.

Let people inside your heart. But ultimately you are the one you have to live with so make sure to be true to you.

A Call to Action:

- Approach your relationships from a place of compassion. Try to understand where the other person is coming from and adapt how you communicate to be most effective.

- Communicate your goals and dreams and allow those closest to support you.
- Limit the amount of time you spend with negative people. Don't allow them to steal your energy. Instead surround yourself with positive, uplifting individuals.

step 4

EXECUTE

What?

"Discontent is the first step in the progress of a man or a nation." —OSCAR WILDE

You've worked your way through discontent to a vision of a better life. Look back through the notes and lists you made in your journal. Compare and review what goals you want to pursue.

Once you know what direction you want to proceed, you need a plan. Many people get to this point then falter. There are several possible reasons for this dilemma with the top two being clarity and fear. Let's begin with overcoming those obstacles.

Clarity: Many people falter because their goal is too broad and unclear. Success comes with clarity. Let's compare. One person has this goal- *I will be rich and famous.* Another person has this goal- *I will have my own internet marketing company that will make one million net profit within two years. My success will put me in high demand as an author and international speaker affording me the pleasure to travel with my family to promote my business.* Who do you believe would be more successful?

When your goal is clear it becomes infinitely easier to know where to focus your efforts. How can you prioritize your actions when you don't know what you want to accomplish?

Remember to include multiple facets of your life when you define your goals. Balance is important to success. Envision your personal life, your relationships, how you want to spend your free time, the specifics of the career of your dreams, how it will fulfill you, the amount of money you want to make, the city you choose to live in, the health and ability you will have to enjoy your success, and anything else you think will help to create a joyful, passionate, balanced life. Write all this down in your journal so you can go back and evaluate and adjust as necessary.

Fear: Fear of failure, success, or the unknown creates barriers. Innumerable doubts cause people to stop taking action. Fear is common. Overcoming fear is not. That is what separates the winners from everyone else. Release your fears and live an abundant life of love, health, wealth, and joy.

"You can live in fear or you can live in love. Choose love." —HEIDI ANDREWS

Look closely at what holds you back and decide if it's a valid obstacle, or an invention of the mind. If doubt is nagging you ask questions. "Who has already done something similar that I can learn from? What would happen if I tried another option to overcoming this challenge? How will this serve me? What do I need to do to make this happen?"

Instead of swimming in fear, turn it around. Begin the day by looking forward to adventure and possibility, not dread. Then stop yourself every time you start to see things in a negative way. Stop complaining. Stop limiting yourself and others around you. Reframe negative talk into positive options. It's contagious and effective. It won't make all of your problems magically disappear but it will clear the way for your mind to create opportunity.

Who?

One of my wonderful coaching clients used to work with me to discuss business issues…marketing, customer service, staffing challenges, etc. After a time he started to sound less enthused about his computer business. I asked him what was going on and he told me that he was frustrated; his business wasn't inspiring him anymore. What got him excited was a class he was teaching on the side.

A discussion uncovered a hidden dream to become a professor. As you can imagine jumping from small business owner to professor required a plan and definitive action. He worked through exactly what would have to happen for his dream to take place and it included massive actions like going back to school for his PhD, selling his business, and somehow making enough money to support his family through this whole process.

The average person might look at this daunting list and say, "I can't do that. It's not practical," then give up and spend the next twenty years merely existing. But my clients aren't average people. They are dreamers of the highest caliber…the kind who make their dreams happen. And the fact that you bought this book makes you a high caliber dreamer too.

My client and I worked together and I'm proud to say that this highly motivated man applied for graduate school, sold his business, stayed on as a consultant to keep a flow of income and create a smoother transition. It took several years but he has graduated and is now living a joyful life of his own creation. With a dream, a plan, and the guts to take action anything is possible.

How?

Taking action is an area that can trip up even the most motivated of individuals. Dreaming is easy. Having the courage to take action on your dreams can be daunting.

"Action is the fundamental key to all success."

—PABLO PICASSO

Let's break down the process into an easy, sensible procedure. Simplicity helps to ensure success.

1. **Define goals.** Start with a big picture then zoom in to view the details. Go back to the visualizations you created from Chapter 2. Then delve deeper. Where do you see yourself in ten years?

What do you want to accomplish? What legacy do you want to leave for future generations? In your journal, write down the specific, measurable goals you have decided will create a new reality…a more joyful, passionate life.

2. **Create a plan.** List the steps that need to take place to achieve success. If your goal is long range your steps may include numerous stages (going back to school, earning and saving a set amount of money to comfortably follow your dreams, finding a mentor, etc)
3. **Prioritize.** Look at your day. Are you taking the time you need for the things that will get you closer to your goal? Prioritize and do the actions that will get you there. Most people spend time putting out fires; responding to the emergencies that occur day in and day out. Instead, create a plan that will prevent the fires from happening. Some emergencies will still occur but when you are clear as to your priorities for achieving your goals there will be time to accomplish at least one step each day to get you closer. Examine your plan and build a timeline of immediacy. What has to happen first on a larger scale as well as what has to happen first each day to make your dreams come true?
4. **Take action** every day. Some days you will take substantial action. But on the days when you have less energy or other things to take care of, it remains imperative to take at least one small action to get you a step closer. Make your dream a priority. Sometimes taking one small step is enough to reinvigorate you to more action. Like throwing a rock into a lake, the ripple effect of a beneficial action will create immeasurable positive repercussions. Action is the only way to get to the desired result. Seizing control

of your destiny may be frightening at first but taking action in spite of your fear is one of the most empowering things you can do. Every single day take a step toward your dream.

Bonus Gems:

Make your objective to follow your dreams known. Put it out there. It's like I mentioned earlier, when you are thinking about buying a product or doing an activity all of a sudden you notice the other people that have done similar things. If you think and talk about your dream, opportunities to make the dream come true will be drawn to you. You will meet helpful people, receive wisdom and advice, and new, exciting chances and prospects will appear. Of course when they do it will be your responsibility to do something about it. Take action.

Take into account your personality, energy, and style when creating a plan. If you are more energized in the morning make sure to schedule the activities that require more thought or liveliness first. Make use of your productive times so that you can be guilt free during times when you need to recharge your batteries.

Celebrate your successes for carrying out your plan for the week. Don't wait until the grand goal is accomplished. Recognize the mini goals with rewards. Just as you would reinforce other's positive behavior with gratitude and appreciation, bolster your energy and accomplishments by patting yourself on the back and other incentives.

Trust yourself. Follow your instincts. Trust that the gut response that is telling you to do something (or not) is there for a reason. Your intuition is one of your most valuable tools. Many people have been taught to disregard it because it is tough to quantify or explain. But in fact your intuition and perception, if encouraged, can be similar to your own internal GPS. It will guide you to the right choices each time.

Surround yourself with the best. Do you play sports better against someone of similar or lesser talent or against someone obviously better than you? People play up. True potential isn't found until you are challenged.

You are the average of the people you spend the most time with. If you want to grow and achieve grander goals than you ever imagined you have to surround yourself with people that have already accomplished big goals. People who are smarter, faster, more positive and highly focused. Their skills will rub off on you and you will get closer to your goal.

Never give up. When I am running and I feel like resting or going home I play a game with myself. I say, "I'll just go to that corner and stop." Then I add another corner and another until I have reached or exceeded my goal. When things are blocking you or you hit a wall of challenges, ask yourself, "If there was a way to make this work…what would it be?" or "If someone had the answer, what would it be?" or "I'll just take this one action and see what happens." Even if the action fails you are that much closer to the goal. You know what doesn't work and you may have revealed an answer you wouldn't have found if you gave up. You can alter your goals; you can change how you get to the end result, but if you know the dream is worthwhile…Never Give Up.

When?

When it comes to taking action everyone from our story has to get on board.

Erin will apply to school, find a new apartment and the courage to stand tall and strong on her own.

Kristy will design a new, healthy lifestyle with more interaction from her husband and friends. She'll learn to take chances like applying for management and ultimately achieve a new level of confidence.

Edward will recreate a life that allows him continued business success while providing more time for family.

Brenda will cultivate her new air of gratitude and recognize the important role she is playing as a mother of three. She'll also be true to herself by appreciating her need for stimulating ideas and brainstorming ways to start her own business.

Joe will take a web design class and have more conversations with Noor about publicizing the message of each person using their unique talent to serve the world.

The concepts the characters discussed are beneficial only to the extent they lead to action. An idea that remains inactive is in the mind or at best in the heart. Action is what will move an idea of the heart to realization and fulfillment.

Why?

Have you ever spoken to someone that experienced regret for a path not taken? Someone that looked back on their life and thought *If only I…?*

Do you have any regrets in your life? It's not too late to make your life better. To have more wealth, health, love, fun, adventure, and joy.

Don't be one of the majority that has a dream but puts it off until some undetermined date in the future. Be part of the select group that follows through and achieves greatness.

When you are tested by self doubt, life's obstacles, negative people, or any number of possible obstructions...dig deep. Anticipate these will happen, plan for them, and deal with even the surprises with a sense of conviction. This is your dream we are talking about. Don't let anyone or anything get in your way!

"Success is not final, failure is not fatal: it is the courage to continue that counts."

—WINSTON CHURCHILL

A Call to Action:

- Create clear, specific, measurable goals and a plan on how to execute them.
- Take action every single day.
- Celebrate your action and your achievements.
- When obstacles occur, make adjustments then take more action. Don't let go of your dreams!

step 5

FIVE—FULL CIRCLE

What?

Right now, it's not about talent and luck. It's about choices. You can do steps one through four and make money doing something fun and interesting. But step five is the one that creates a legacy. It's the one that is slightly harder and infinitely more rewarding. It's the one that people will talk about at your eulogy.

Don't think of limitations. Think of possibilities. When you ask yourself *Am I all I can be?* what is your answer? What can you give back, teach, contribute, or add to the world? Nothing will make you feel as complete as when you are fulfilling your destiny. In order to fulfill your destiny something of yourself needs to be left behind.

"Live in the service of something higher and more enduring, so that when the tragic transience of life at last breaks in upon you, you can feel that the thing for which you have lived does not die." —GILBERT MURRAY

Think of a story that has touched your heart. Is it about selfishness or generosity? Aren't the best stories about helping, giving, and loving? About ordinary people doing extraordinary things? About courage and strength and hope?

How do you go from ordinary to extraordinary? You step beyond yourself.

Some of the greatest minds, the most heroic actions, the most extraordinary deeds came from surprising sources. Thomas Edison was one of seven children, had only three months of official schooling, and had severe hearing difficulties due to a bout of Scarlet Fever. He also had over 1,000 patents and his experimentation with the generation of electricity was life changing.

Helen Keller, due to childhood illness, became deaf and blind by the age of three. She was the first deaf and blind person to earn a Bachelor of Arts degree and went on to become a prolific author and activist.

Elie Wiesel and his family were sent to the German concentration camps during World War II. He made the decision to use his experience, not to foster hatred, but to write of the moral responsibility of all to fight hatred. Political activist, author, and Nobel Peace Prize winner…he implored untold numbers to do the right thing.

John F. Kennedy was a sickly child with illness after illness in his early years. Several doctors who informed his parents he would not last the year were, in all probability, astounded when he became the youngest elected president, as well as an advocate for civil rights, foreign affairs, and arguably one of the most articulate and inspirational presidential orators of our time.

J.K. Rowling was a single mother on welfare when her first Harry Potter book was published. She poured the pain of her mother's death and financial worries into her books creating a series that became an unparalleled success, with each of the seven books being within the top 15 best sellers of all time. This success provided her with the means to establish a trust to help combat poverty. Rowling said, "I think you have a moral responsibility when you've been given far more than you need, to do wise things with it and give intelligently." (USA Today, 2003)

Ghandi, Nelson Mandela, Mother Theresa…the list goes on and on of ordinary people overcoming great odds to bring something extraordinary to the world.

Who?

One day a good friend, and associate was telling me about this big project he wanted to pursue. We often help each other achieve our business goals with accountability. Many people had already told Croix he was crazy, that "it was impossible" and he should try something "more realistic." His idea? He wanted to run across America in 100 days. When he saw me nodding he continued. He said he also wanted to give a speech each day to inspire teens and adults in underserved communities to follow their dreams. He was planning to run across the country and inspire a nation.

Many people he had told thought *that will never work* but I heard him and thought *that's fantastic*. I turned to him and said, "You HAVE to do this!" I was thinking of the amazing gift he would be giving himself and hundreds of thousands of people and what a loss it would be if this inspired action never took place. As of publication Croix Sather, of Dream Big Act Big, is in training and will begin his run across America in February of 2011.

Every so often you have to step beyond ordinary and do something crazy. Shake up the world, take a chance, and make a difference.

How?

Everyone is different. People have different intentions, motivations, and ways of looking at the world. What works for one will not work for all.

Here you will find a series of stages that should give everyone of every comfort level the opportunity to step in the direction of creating a legacy. Some will jump straight in the pool while others will dip their toes. No judgments here. Wherever you are now, you can get closer to a higher level of consciousness regarding your impact on the world.

Baby Steps–If you aren't a massive action, jump out of a plane kind of person, no words of mine on the benefits of extreme living will connect. But that doesn't mean that you can't achieve your dreams. It means that you need to take smaller steps. Quitting your high paying corporate job to build birdhouses when you have a family to support may not make the most sense. However existing day to day in continued misery is not the answer. Baby steps are the answer. To continue with the example, you can build birdhouses on the side. The act of doing what you love without pay will still bring you joy.

For those that believe they don't have the time to do something on the side, you might want to consider how much more energy you will have doing something you love instead of sitting on the couch watching TV. Everyone has the same amount of time. You can choose to fill yours with escapism or with a progressive step to making a difference in the world.

Eventually your birdhouses could draw the attention of friends, family and others and you could turn it into that business you wanted.

Childlike–The next stage over baby steps is a willingness to live a childlike existence. Children have the most genuine ability to live in the moment. Every adult I know can benefit from the wisdom of a child's wonder and joyful exuberance. Whatever your current situation, however stressful, taking time to connect with nature, play with your kids, smile at a friend, or notice the beauty of each moment will recharge your batteries. Play is important to retaining a youthful vitality at any age.

Do one random act of kindness each day (such as holding a door, giving a sweater to someone who is cold, or being there for a friend in need with no ulterior motive). If you want to make real change contemplate the possibility of a life that includes all of the most beautiful aspects of existence on a regular basis.

Living a compassionate life filled with play, gratitude, and loving kindness will impact everyone with whom you come in contact.

Adolescent–What comes to mind when you think of adolescence? Change. Do you want to go above the basic stages? Do you want to make real change? It won't be comfortable. But I'm not here to tell you that comfort is the best thing out there. Challenge, love, beauty, joy, hope, excitement, curiosity, these are powerful motivators. Look at yourself and ask, "What do I need to change to be a better person?" Be honest.

I know I could be more patient and compassionate. I spend time daily working on strategies to improve in this area. Deep breathing, meditation, gratitude lists, and self induced time outs to name a few. Perfection is not the goal. Striving to do the right thing and focusing on bettering yourself will not only help you, it will help those around you by your example. Make yourself a priority. Be willing to change, grow, and love yourself in the process.

Adult–This stage is about using what you do for a living to give back.

For example, let's assume you are a teacher in a small town. If you are the best possible you, and not only impart your wisdom, but a piece of your heart, by being the type of teacher that sees a child for who he or she really is…and encourages them to greatness...you become so much more. One of your students could go on to be a politician that advocates for world peace, or a movie director that influences the masses with positive, constructive messages, or a doctor that heals and strengthens many…you get the idea.

Perhaps your dream involves music. You could decide to leave your corporate job to handcraft violins. You put all of who you are into your craft and one of your masterpieces calls out to the next musical prodigy. Music from his or her hands could inspire thousands.

Not to say everyone should go off and leave the corporate world. It's a matter of bringing joy to whatever you decide to do. Maybe you will rise up the corporate ladder, become a CEO of a pharmaceutical company that ends up discovering the cure for cancer.

If you are going through transition and are making changes in your career, it is the perfect time to think about how you can fully realize your potential and make the biggest impact on those around you. Take the time to contemplate the imprint your existence will make on others. Create your legacy.

Professional–This final level of the stages is professional because it is the point where you go beyond, do something extraordinary, and find a way to create a cycle of abundance that benefits you, your family, the community, and the world. This is massive action.

Bill Gates left Harvard University to start a computer software company with Paul Allen. Microsoft made Gates one of the richest men in America. But did he hoard it all or spend with complete indiscretion? No, he created one of the largest charitable organizations in the world, giving well over $38 billion dollars to charity. Massive charitable action.

Paul Newman was an actor of the highest caliber, winning an Academy Award, an Emmy and three Golden Globes to name a few. But did he stop and revel in his success to the detriment of others? No. He started the food company Newman's Own and donated all post tax profits to charity, over $300 million at publication.

You don't have to make millions or billions to deliver true impact on the world. You do have to crave a whole new level of existence and generosity. You have to give of yourself.

My past life was that of a dancer and actor and I had this idea to find a way to give back by incorporating performance. I created a night of the arts to benefit a local charity. Dancers, singers, speakers, and musicians donated their time and local businesses donated goods for the auction. The night was filled with inspiration, the audience loved it, and the charity received thousands. Anyone can take something they are passionate about and incorporate a way to give back.

The benefits to serving others will create a cycle of positive energy. In addition, paying it forward will teach others a new habit- a new pattern of living that is far superior to the egocentric path upon which the world is headed.

> **"Everybody can be great…because anybody can serve. You don't have to have a college degree to serve. You don't have to make your subject and verb agree to serve. You only need a heart full of grace. A soul generated by love."** —MARTIN LUTHER KING, JR.

Now is the time to move forward. Let's sum up what we've learned.

Fire in 5 process:

Freedom–Take back control of your life.

I am–Discover your unique gifts.

Reaching out–Understand the importance that relationships play in your success.

Execute–Define the plan and take action!

FIVE–Come full circle- reach a higher level of consciousness by using your unique talent to serve the world.

Take out that journal you've been writing in and make a new list. Write down all the people, causes, and projects that are near and dear to your heart. Go back to your previous work. Look at what you excel at, what you enjoy doing, and figure out how you can marry the lists. What unique talent do you have that will enable you to benefit the most people? How can you serve?

When?

From Chapter 6, a few of the characters took the concept of giving back or paying it forward to heart.

Joe will help Noor spread his message and perhaps even make a business of helping other non-profits expand public awareness of their message. And Erin will be an inspirational example for women to find their inner strength.

All the characters of the story made their way through self centered direction and began looking beyond themselves. By the end they all grasped that finding and living a more joyful life isn't selfish because it demonstrates vitality. Beyond that the idea of using their unique gifts to help others generated a positive energy that will sustain them during their mission.

Why?

Follow your dreams and create a magic that empowers your true path to serving others and will inspire those around you. In addition to directly encouraging others to follow their dreams, there are many ways to give back.

You can donate your time, material things, or money to a worthy charity. You can use your talents to build a house, mentor a child, help with fundraising, visit someone lonely in a hospital, or educate people on the perils of drunk driving. There are vast numbers of opportunities to assist those in need. Get creative and find something that speaks to you and gets you excited and energized. Finding a balance of fun, focused effort, and giving back is imperative to successfully generate a complete picture.

There are so many ways to leave a legacy. A small gesture to help and encourage someone with less opportunity could be planting a seed. That person could go on to help another…who could go on to help thousands. Many times we never know the impact we are making. Living a life of joy and hope and love will affirm and influence those around you. Like the domino, a small action can create ripples of positive effects for years to come.

Stop and Ask Yourself:

What do I want to leave behind? What do I want people to say when they think of me? What is my legacy?

How do we have the courage to uncover all we can accomplish? Sometimes it requires tough decisions. The definition of courage is "the ability to face danger, difficulty, uncertainty, or pain without being overcome by fear or being deflected from a chosen course of action." The difference between ordinary and extraordinary is the ability to take action when things are hard. The ability to have the courage to do what we know is right and good. The ability to follow our dreams and make a difference in the world…for even just one person at a time.

Sometimes time, money, and effort needs to be extended to get to the place of fulfillment. But you know you are on the right path when the extra time and money is giving you energy. If you feel tired, scared, lonely, or discontent you are on the wrong path. If you feel energized and excited you are headed in the right direction. Life is meant to be lived to the fullest. Too many people live half lives…existing day to day without joy and without contributing to a better purpose. Find the passion in life. The world deserves what you have to offer and you deserve to feel the contentment and satisfaction that comes from doing all you can do.

A Call to Action:

- Live the life you love, enjoy every precious moment, and you will spread inspiration to those around you.
- Decide how you can take your message, your unique talent, to a wider audience. Take action to make that happen today.
- Write a letter to your grandchildren (I understand they may not yet exist), a school, or some other young person or organization that will be around in the future. Make a promise of what you hope to accomplish. Writing the letter is a commitment to follow through on your goals to improve an aspect of the world for them.

You could think of a million reasons why you shouldn't share the unique beauty that makes you special. But think of all the people that would benefit from seeing and feeling that beauty. Would you deprive them of that? Would you deprive yourself of the overwhelming experience and joy to all senses to give that kind of gift?

Go, Be, Do...Create a legacy. Find your fire and share it with the world.

epilogue

One year later…

It was a warm April day. The sun was sparkling on the pond like thousands of fireflies. Joe was sitting on the bench tapping lightly on his keyboard as Edward strolled up, "Hey Joe. How are you, buddy?"

"Edward, great to see you. Let me finish shutting this down and we can talk." Edward took a seat on the bench, closed his eyes and listened to the caw of the birds and the children laughing. It was a good idea to meet in the park.

Snapping his laptop closed Joe said, "You look good. How are you?"

"I'm great. I brought my family along to meet everyone. See that beautiful brunette playing with the little blond dude waving like a mad man? That's them." Edward grinned and waved at his son.

"I'm happy for you. Oh, here comes Kristy."

Kristy ran up and hugged Joe then Edward, "Aren't you two a sight for sore eyes? I've missed you both."

Edward said, "Who are you? And what have you done with Kristy? My God, woman, you look amazing!"

Kristy blushed and said, "Always the charmer, Edward. I did lose a little weight and a lot of baggage. How have you both been?"

"Really Kristy, not just the weight, you always looked good…but something about you is different. It's almost like a light has been turned on and is shining out of you." Joe stammered.

"Thank you, Joe. That means a lot. You look good too." Kristy smiled at Joe's discomfort and Edward tried to save him by asking, "Erin and Brenda are meeting us here, right? Then we'll walk over together?"

Joe said, "Yes, isn't that Brenda now? Her little monkeys are a dead giveaway."

Ian and Zach were exuberantly climbing on every rock they passed. One of them was wielding a stick that appeared heavier than the boy's own body weight. Meanwhile Sophie was quietly walking beside her mom picking the petals off the daisies she carried in her little fist.

Edward said, "Stroller days are over, huh Brenda?"

"As you can see," Brenda pointed to her mud covered sons. "Laundry has increased since they started walking."

As Brenda gave hugs all around Kristy asked, "You weren't at dance class last week. What happened?"

Brenda replied, "Steven had to work late and my sitter backed out. I'll be there next week."

Erin approached, with pointer finger to her lips so the others wouldn't give her away, snuck up behind Edward and placed her hands over his eyes, "Guess who?"

He turned and gave her a big hug over the bench. At that point his wife and son walked over. "Hello."

Edward made introductions all around. Smiling graciously, his wife Elizabeth hugged each person and said, "So this is the crew that made such a transformation of my Edward." Then she faced Erin, "May I talk with you for a moment?"

All the light hearted laughter ceased and an uncomfortable silence descended on the group. "Um. Sure." The two walked ahead to where an older couple was throwing bread crumbs to a cluster of Mallards.

Elizabeth noticed Erin's white face and tense jaw and decided to put her at ease. "No worries, Erin. I'm here to thank you." Seeing her shocked expression Elizabeth continued, "Before what Edward and I refer to as "the day of the storm" I was seriously considering divorce."

Surprised Erin said, "What!"

"It's true. I've always loved Edward but we had gotten to a place of such animosity in our marriage it was painful. I hated what a nagging witch I had turned into just to make him see me." Laughing Elizabeth added, "He hated it too!"

"When he came home from the coffee shop that evening he was… different. I remember he had gotten a sitter to take me out to dinner the next day and I thought *here it comes*. But it wasn't what I expected. He tried to explain about the bizarre conversation you all had during the storm, but I'm not sure I ever really understood. All I know is that he poured his heart out. He told me about you and how attracted he was to you and that you were very brave. At first I wanted to kill you, I mean the fact that my husband was passionately kissing a hot redhead and telling me about it did not initially fill me with a wealth of good feeling toward you. But after I realized the change in him was permanent, I wanted to thank you. He's sweet, helpful, appreciative, and he spends time planning special things for us to do as a family. Brian has been on cloud nine. Frankly, so have I. You and that crazy gang of yours over there saved our marriage. Thank you. You should know that Edward voluntarily avoided going back to the Coffee Encounter just because he wanted me to feel comfortable knowing that he was not pursuing anything with you. I didn't ask him to do that, but his suggesting it was a big part of winning me over to believing he really wanted to make a change."

With tears in her eyes, Erin gave her a big, bear hug. "I'm happy for you both. Edward is a wonderful man and he loves you so much."

The two women walked back to a group that appeared to have been holding their breath for the last several minutes.

Elizabeth said, "I'll leave you now to your reunion. It was a pleasure meeting all of you. Come on Brian." She kissed Edward and walked away.

Brenda said, "What just happened?"

Edward replied, "Elizabeth thinks I'm somehow different and she wanted to meet you. Especially you, Erin. I hope you don't mind that I told her about us."

Erin said, "It was the only way for you two to reconnect properly. I'm glad you did. She's lovely."

Edward nodded, "Yes, she is. So are we ready to head to Coffee Encounter and see our buddy?"

Whoops and shouts all around. They walked and caught each other up to date on their lives.

Erin had trained to become a domestic violence hot line worker and was receiving valuable experience while working on her Master's Degree in counseling. She had rented an apartment with another woman from her college and was thoroughly enjoying her newfound independence.

She also acknowledged that for a while she had consciously avoided the Coffee Encounter because Paul had often gone there looking for her, so she stayed away from places she thought she might see him.

Kristy had tried to work things out with her husband Frank but found they had little in common with the children out of the house. They were separated and she was living with her sister and often babysat for her two nieces. Not only had she acquired that management position at her company but she was now in charge of the entire east coast training department. She loved every minute of it, very busy with less time for things like a relaxed latte at the Coffee Encounter, but fulfilling.

Brenda was excited to tell the group about her new plan. She had been receiving so many compliments on her kids' eco-friendly birthday parties as well as her creative ideas for moms' night out that she decided to look into environmental party planning. She explained that the idea was still in its infancy but was looking forward to researching it and designing the business plan. By the time the kids were in school she expected to be up and running. Steven was encouraging and they were both looking forward to their first vacation alone together in years. They had booked a cruise to the Caribbean for next month.

And there he was now. She saw Steven coming toward them down the street and felt that familiar tingle in her heart. She was lucky. "Hi Honey. Thanks for taking the kids so I can have some coffee with the gang."

"Anything for the gang…hello everybody," As Steven tried to meet everyone, Ian was pulling his pants leg. Sophie kept say, "Daisies, Daddy, Daisies!" And when Zach got loose and tried to run Steven gave up, waved and took the kids home. Brenda smiled.

Kristy asked, "Have you had much luck with the web design idea, Joe?"

"Thanks for asking. I took this intense online design program. It was amazing. I have more to tell but we're here. Let's hook up with Noor and we can explain together. With taking the class and looking for opportunities, I hardly ever get to hang around the Coffee Encounter." He held the door open for her. Everyone walked in then stopped in surprise. They had never seen so many people here before. The place was packed.

Noticing Noor clearing tables nearby Brenda asked, "What's going on here?"

"Hey guys! It's great to see you. What happened? He happened." Noor beamed and pointed at Joe.

Joe looked at the floor and grinned. "It was a joint effort."

Kristy said, "Look at that line."

"Good thing you know somebody, then. Find a seat and I'll bring your drinks to the table. What will you have?"

Edward said, "Come on. Let's make it easy on him. How about five coffees? Wait, Joe drinks tea. Four coffees and a tea?" Everyone nodded and Noor headed behind the counter.

They found a table by the window. Edward was about to sit next to Kristy but upon noticing the look in Joe's eye, moved over and let him sit in his spot. Joe radiated gratitude.

Noor returned with steaming mugs and a tray of croissants, "Update me, guys. What's been going on?"

They each told their story of how much their day together impacted them and of all the ways they have changed and grown. None of them had been at the Coffee Encounter as regularly recently, and this was the first time Erin or Edward had been in the place in months. Noor was as proud as a parent to hear of all they had accomplished.

Erin said, "I still can't believe how many people are here."

"Amazing, isn't it? It's been packed like this since the website went live. In addition to the locals here I get requests to open locations in other cities every day. I haven't gotten that far yet but I've started traveling around to meet with small groups interested in the message. Joe's certainly got a knack for getting the word out."

Kristy patted Joe on the back and said, "I can't wait to see this website!"

Brenda said, "Think of all those people finding their fire and sharing their gifts with the world. It gives me chills. It's just like you talked about last year. You made it happen."

"So did all of you," Noor replied.

Even though the sky was clear and the door was ajar, the six friends felt as if they had been transported back to that special day. They laughed and talked for hours.

Edward, Erin, Joe, Brenda, Kristy and Noor were grateful. Noor was grateful for good friends and a beating heart. The rest were grateful Noor was still alive and well and living each day as if it were his last…a living and breathing example for us all.

about the author

HEATHER HANSEN O'NEILL is the president of Progressive Image and creator of the Fire in Five program. She is an award winning speaker, author, and coach presenting to organizations and corporations on transition, change, and joyful living.

Heather walks her talk everyday by living a life she loves... rock climbing, skydiving, wind surfing, professional dancing, and competitive running. She runs a successful business transforming lives and companies while making plenty of quality time for raising her three high-energy boys.

She currently lives with her family in Connecticut.

For more information on her live events,
one-on-one coaching, webinars,
books, CDs and DVDs visit
www.findyourfireinfive.com
or call 888-828-3890

special bonus
Offer for Book Buyers

Because I want each reader to get the most from the strategies in this book, I am offering an exceptional audio special. Go to **www.FindYourFireInFive.com/bookbonus**, input your name and email address and you will receive an email to download your free Find Your Fire audio file (regularly priced $49.95). This special program is only for book buyers and will provide reinforcement exercises, new stories and a bonus three steps to help you find your fire!

Would you like your employees to have a burning desire to come to work? Ask about the Find Your Fire corporate keynotes and workshops and receive $300 off when you mention this book. The number to call is 888-828-3890.

Go To www.findyourfireinfive.com Today!

Each person who downloads this bonus will be entered into a drawing each month to **win a complimentary** 45 minute coaching session valued at **$500**

BUY A SHARE OF THE FUTURE IN YOUR COMMUNITY

These certificates make great holiday, graduation and birthday gifts that can be personalized with the recipient's name. The cost of one S.H.A.R.E. or one square foot is $54.17. The personalized certificate is suitable for framing and will state the number of shares purchased and the amount of each share, as well as the recipient's name. The home that you participate in "building" will last for many years and will continue to grow in value.

Here is a sample SHARE certificate:

HABITAT FOR HUMANITY

THIS CERTIFIES THAT

YOUR NAME HERE

HAS INVESTED IN A HOME FOR A DESERVING FAMILY

1985-2005

TWENTY YEARS OF BUILDING FUTURES IN OUR COMMUNITY ONE HOME AT A TIME

1200 SQUARE FOOT HOUSE @ $65,000 = $54.17 PER SQUARE FOOT

This certificate represents a tax deductible donation. It has no cash value.

YES, I WOULD LIKE TO HELP!

I support the work that Habitat for Humanity does and I want to be part of the excitement! As a donor, I will receive periodic updates on your construction activities but, more importantly, I know my gift will help a family in our community realize the dream of homeownership. ***I would like to SHARE in your efforts against substandard housing in my community!*** *(Please print below)*

PLEASE SEND ME ___________ SHARES at $54.17 EACH = $ $___________

In Honor Of: ______________________________

Occasion: *(Circle One)* *HOLIDAY* *BIRTHDAY* *ANNIVERSARY*

OTHER: ______________________________

Address of Recipient: ______________________________

Gift From: _______________ ***Donor Address:*** _______________

Donor Email: ______________________________

I AM ENCLOSING A CHECK FOR $ $_____________ PAYABLE TO HABITAT FOR HUMANITY <u>OR</u> PLEASE CHARGE MY VISA OR MASTERCARD *(CIRCLE ONE)*

Card Number ______________________ Expiration Date: ___________

Name as it appears on Credit Card _______________ Charge Amount $ ___________

Signature ______________________________

Billing Address ______________________________

Telephone # Day ___________________ Eve ___________________

PLEASE NOTE: Your contribution is tax-deductible to the fullest extent allowed by law.

Habitat for Humanity • P.O. Box 1443 • Newport News, VA 23601 • 757-596-5553

www.HelpHabitatforHumanity.org

Printed in the USA
CPSIA information can be obtained
at www.ICGtesting.com
JSHW081959070224
56875JS00002B/211

9 781600 379017

ON

ldren who enjoy the world of birds as much as I do.

LEDGMENTS

nks to the National Wildlife Refuge System along with state gencies, both public and private, for stewarding the lands itical to the many bird species we so love.

Sandy Livoti
d book design by Jonathan Norberg
ions by Elleyna Ruud
maps produced by Anthony Hertzel

photos by Stan Tekiela: Roseate Spoonbill, Florida Scrub-Jay, ern Cardinal, Painted Bunting, American Oystercatcher, Osprey Double-crested Cormorant

otos by Stan Tekiela except p. 56 (main) by **Agami Photo Agency/Shutterstock.com;** 8 (cap) by **Steve Byland/Shutterstock.com;** pg. 168 (belly) by **Dennis W. Donohue/ terstock.com;** pp. 124 (wings) and 174 (wings) by **Dudley Edmondson;** pg. 146 (head) by **inda Fawver/Shutterstock.com;** pg. 206 (feet) by **Phil Friar/Shutterstock.com;** pg. 57 by **otte Rusty Harold/Shutterstock.com;** pg. 102 (bill) by **Ray Hennessy/Shutterstock.com;** . 171 by **Dennis Jacobsen/Shutterstock.com;** pg. 146 (main) by **Frode Jacobsen/Shutterstock. m;** pp. 56 (belly) and 200 (winter) by **Kevin T. Karlson;** pg. 35 by **Brendan Klick;** pg. 97 by **Maslowski Wildlife Productions;** p. 102 (main) by **Paul Reeves Photography/Shutterstock. com;** pg. 228 by **Dr. Pixel/Shutterstock.com;** pg. 38 (inset) by **Nickolay Stanev/Shutterstock. com;** pg. 103 by **vagabond54/Shutterstock.com;** pg. 166 (wings) by **Hartmut Walter;** pg. 40 (juvenile) by **Brian K. Wheeler;** and pg. 96 (side) by **Jim Zipp**

To the best of the publisher's knowledge, all photos were of live birds. Some were photographed in a controlled condition.

10 9 8 7 6 5 4

The Kids' Guide to Birds of Florida: Fun Facts, Activities and 87 Cool Birds

Published by Adventure Publications
An imprint of AdventureKEEN
310 Garfield Street South
Cambridge, Minnesota 55008
(800) 678-7006
www.adventurepublications.net

Printed in the United States of America
ISBN 978-1-59193-835-4 (pbk.); ISBN 978-1-59193-836-1 (ebook)

Bir… Flori…

Fun Facts, Acti… and 87 Cool Bir…

DEDICATI…

To all the chi…

ACKNOW…

Special tha…
and local a…
that are cr…

Edited by…
Cover a…
Illustra…
Range…

Cover…
North…
and…

All p…
pg. 1…

by Stan Tekiela

Adventure Publications
Cambridge, Minnesota

Quick-Flip Color Guide

TABLE OF CONTENTS

Introduction

The Birds

Bird Food Fun for the Family

COOL BIRDS IN FLORIDA

The Kids' Guide to Birds of Florida is a fun, easy-to-use guide for anyone interested in seeing and identifying birds. As a child, I spent hours of enjoyment watching birds come to a wooden feeder that my father built in our backyard. We were the only family in the neighborhood who fed birds, and we became known as the nature family.

Now, more people feed birds in their backyards than those who go hunting or fishing combined. Not only has it become very popular to feed and watch birds, but young and old alike are also identifying them and learning more about them.

Florida is a fantastic place to see all sorts of birds. In fact, more than 500 species are found here! That makes it one of the top states to watch an incredible variety of birds. In this field guide for Florida, I'm featuring 87 of the most common of these great species.

We have marvelous habitats in Florida that are perfect for birds. Each **habitat** supports different kinds of birds. Ocean surrounds most of the state. Beaches and rocky shores are wonderful places to see a wide variety of shorebirds, such as Brown Pelicans, and wading birds, such as Snowy Egrets. Florida also has extensive forests, which are home to many smaller songbirds, like Brown Nuthatches.

Florida has lots of **deciduous** forest habitats! Birds that prefer this habitat are often bright and colorful, and they build nests in leafy trees.

In addition, we have a lot of ponds, rivers and lakes. These freshwater environments are home to Ring-necked Ducks, Roseate Spoonbills, Great Blue Herons, White Ibis and more.

The seasons here also play a role in the kinds of birds we see. Carolina Wrens, Monk Parakeets and many more birds nest here during summer. Migrating shorebirds, such as Ruddy Turnstones and Sanderlings, come to Florida for our warm winters. A wide array of other birds, including Sandhill Cranes and Bald Eagles, live here all year long. On top of that, backyard birds, most notably buntings, bluebirds and cardinals, enjoy our seasons year-round.

As you can see, Florida is a terrific place to watch all kinds of cool birds. It is my sincere hope that you and your family will like watching and feeding birds as much as I did with my family when I was a kid. Let this handy book guide you into a lifetime of appreciating birds and nature.

BODY BASICS OF A BIRD

It's good to know the names of a bird's body parts. The right terminology will help you describe and identify a bird when you talk about it with your friends and family.

The basic parts of a bird are labeled in the illustration below. The drawing is a combination (composite) of several birds and should not be regarded as one particular species.

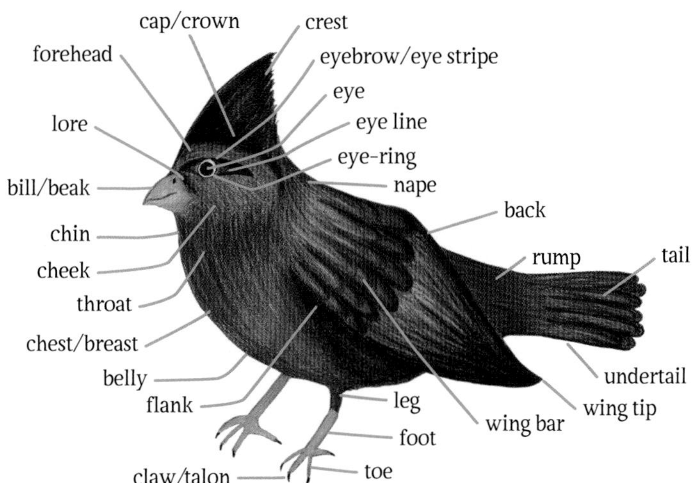

AMAZING NESTS

I am fascinated with bird nests! They are amazing structures that do more than just provide a place for egg laying. Nests create a small climate-controlled environment that's beneficial for both keeping the eggs warm and raising the young after they hatch.

From the high treetops to the ground, there are many kinds of nests. Some are simple, while others are complex. In any case, they function in nearly the same way. Nests help to contain the eggs so they don't roll away. They also help to keep baby birds warm on cold nights, cool on hot days and dry during rains.

The following illustrations show the major types of nests that birds build in Florida.

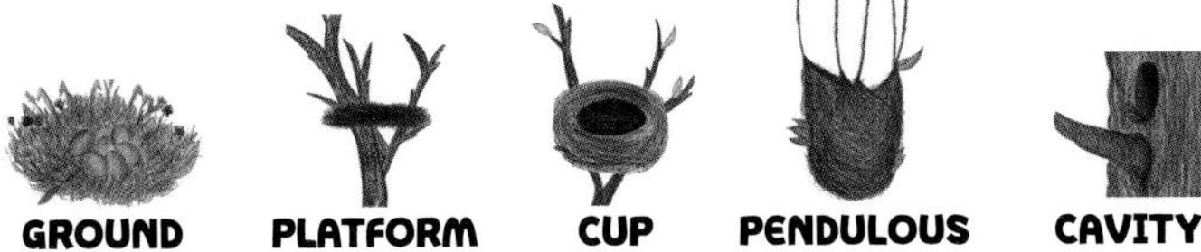

A **ground nest** can be a mound of plant materials on the ground or in the water. Some are just a shallow spot scraped in the earth.

A **platform nest** is a cluster of sticks with a depression in the center. It is secured to the platform of a tree fork, or to several tree branches.

A **cup nest** has a cupped interior, like a bowl.

A **pendulous nest** is a woven nest that hangs and swings freely, like a pendulum, from a branch.

A **cavity nest** is simply a cavity, or hole, usually in a tree.

The first step in nest building is to choose an appropriate site. Each bird species has a unique requirement for this. Some birds, such as American Robins, just need a tree branch. Others, like Eastern Bluebirds, look for a cavity and build the nest inside. Still others, such as Killdeer, search for camouflaged ground to scrape out a nest. Sometimes birds, like Turkey Vultures, don't bother building a nest at all if they spot a hard-to-reach cliff or rocky ledge, where it will be safe to lay their eggs.

Nest materials usually consist of common natural items found in the area, like sticks or dried grass. Birds use other materials, such as mud or spiderwebs, to glue the materials together.

One of the amazing things about nest construction is that the parents don't need building plans or tool belts. They already know by instinct how to build nests, and they use their beaks and feet as their main tools.

To bring in nesting materials, birds must make many trips back and forth to the nest site. Most use their beaks to hold as much material as possible during each trip. Some of the bigger birds, like Ospreys, use larger materials, such as thick sticks and thin branches. They grasp and carry these items with their feet.

Nest building can take two to four days or longer, depending on the species and nest type. The simpler the nest, the faster the construction. Mourning Dove parents, for example, take just a few days to collect one to two dozen sticks for their platform nest. Woodpecker pairs, however, work upwards of a week to **excavate**, or dig out, a suitable nesting cavity. Large and more complicated platform nests, such as a Bald Eagle nest, may take weeks or even a month to complete, but these can be used for years and are worth the extra effort.

WHO BUILT THAT NEST?

In the majority of bird species, the chief builder is the female. In other species, both the female and the male typically share in the construction equally.

In general, when male and female birds look vastly different, the female does most of the work. When the male and female look alike or appear very similar, they tend to share the tasks of nest building and feeding the young. Alternatively, some species of woodpeckers have a different building plan. When they chisel out a nesting chamber, often the male does more of the work after the female has chosen the site.

ATTRACTING BIRDS WITH FEEDERS

To get more birds to visit your yard, an easy way to invite them is to put out bird feeders. Bird feeders are often as unique as the birds themselves, so the types of feeders you use really depends on the kinds of birds you're trying to attract.

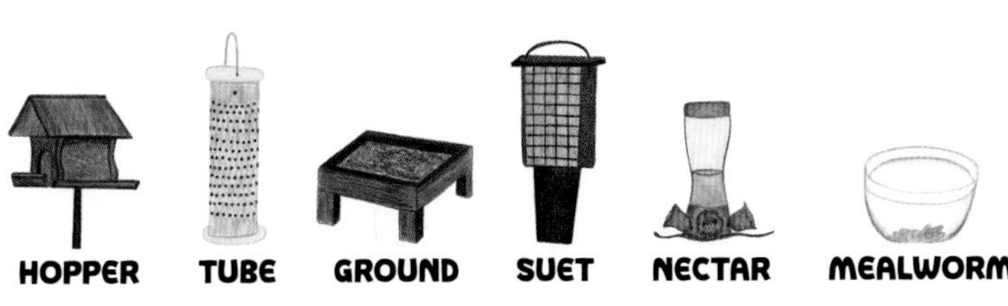

Hopper feeders are often wooden or plastic. Designed to hold a large amount of seeds, they often have a slender opening along the bottom, which dispenses the seeds. Birds land along the sides and help themselves to the food. Hopper feeders work well as main feeders in conjunction with other types of feeders. They are perfect for offering several kinds of seed mixes for cardinals, finches, nuthatches, chickadees and more.

Tube feeders with large seed ports and multiple perches are very popular. Often mostly plastic, they tend to be rugged enough to last several years and can be easily cleaned. These feeders are great for black oil sunflower seeds and seed mixes, which are favorites of cardinals and all the other bird species that also visit hopper feeders.

Some tube feeders have small holes, allowing incredibly tiny thistle seeds to be dispensed just a few at a time. Use this kind of feeder to offer Nyjer seed, which will attract various finches.

Other styles of tube feeders have a wire mesh covering with openings large enough for birds to extract one of their favorite foods—peanuts out of the shell. Most birds enjoy peanuts, so these feeders will be some of the most popular in your yard. Another variety of tube feeder has openings large enough for peanuts in the shell. These are also very popular with the birds.

Ground feeders allow a wide variety of birds to access the food. The simplest and easiest feeders to use, they consist of a flat platform with a lip around the edges to keep seeds and corn from spilling out. Some have a roof to keep rain and snow off the food. With or without a roof, drainage holes in the bottom are important. Ground feeders will bring in towhees and many other birds to your backyard, including doves, and even mallards if you're near water.

Suet feeders are simply wire cages that hold cakes of **suet**. The wire allows woodpeckers, nuthatches and other birds to cling securely to the feeder while pecking out chunks of suet. The best suet feeders have a vertical extension at the bottom where a woodpecker can brace its tail and support itself while feeding. These are called tail-prop suet feeders.

Nectar feeders are glass or plastic containers that hold sugar water. These feeders usually have plastic parts that are bright red, a color that is extremely attractive to hummingbirds, but orioles and woodpeckers will also stop for a drink. They often have up to four ports for access to the liquid and yellow bee guards to prevent bees from getting inside.

Mealworm feeders can be very basic—a simple glass or plastic cup or container will do. Pick one with sides tall enough and make sure the material is slippery enough to stop the lively mealworms from crawling out. Bluebirds especially love this wiggly treat!

HOW TO USE THIS GUIDE

Birds move pretty fast, so you don't often get a lot of time to observe them. To help you quickly find the birds in the book, this guide is organized by color. Simply note the most prominent color of the bird you've seen. A Pileated Woodpecker, for example, is black and white and has a red crest. Since this bird is mostly black and white, you would find it in the black and white section.

Within each color section, the birds are organized by size, from small to large. Use the Real Quick sidebar to find the size that your bird appears to be.

When the male and female of a species are different colors (like the Northern Shoveler pair below), they are shown in their own color sections. In these cases, the opposite sex is included in an inset photo with a page reference so you can easily turn to it.

If you already know the name of the bird you've seen, use the checklist/index to get the page number and flip to it to learn more about the bird.

To further help you with identification, check the range maps to see where and when the bird you have sighted is normally in Florida. Range maps capture our current knowledge of where the birds are during a given year (presence) but do not indicate how many birds are in the area (density). In addition, since birds fly around freely, it's possible to see them outside of their ranges. So please use the maps to get a general idea of where the birds are most likely to be seen.

For more about the information given for each bird in this guide, turn to the Indigo Bunting sample on pp. 16–17.

While you're learning about birds and identifying them, don't forget to check out the fun-filled things to do starting on pg. 220. Score a big hit with the birds in your yard by creating tasty treats or making your own bird food from the recipes. Put out some nesting materials to help birds build their nests. Consider signing up for a cool citizen science project suitable for the entire family. These are just a few of the activities that are such great fun, you'll want to do them all!

Indigo Bunting

Common name

Look for the vibrant blue feathers

MALE

Colored border shows the color section of the opposite sex

Turn to the page number to see the opposite sex of the species

FEMALE

pg. 93

What to look for:

outstanding features; may include other plumages and descriptions

Where you'll find them:

where you're most likely to see the bird

Calls and songs:

songs, calls and other sounds the bird makes

On the move:

anything about flight, flocks, travel and other movements

What they eat:

foods the bird eats and the kinds of feeders it visits

Nest:

type of nest; may include nest site, materials and more

Eggs, chicks and childcare:

number of eggs, color and marks; **incubation** and feeding duties; may include how many broods

Spends the winter:

where the bird goes when it's cold or when food is scarce

Color tab — **Mostly Blue**

REAL QUICK

Length from head to tail — Size $5\frac{1}{2}$"

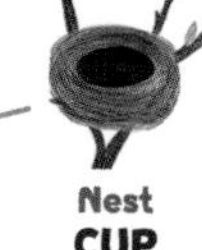

Type of nest the bird calls home — Nest **CUP**

Type of feeder the bird generally visits — Feeder **HOPPER**

Range map — year-round, summer, migration, winter

The bold word means it is defined in the glossary

After you've seen it, checkmark it — **SAW IT!**

STAN'S COOL STUFF

Fun and interesting facts about the bird. Information not typically found in other field guides.

Eastern Towhee

Look for the black head

MALE

FEMALE
pg. 97

What to look for:
mostly black bird with rusty sides, a white belly, white eyes, and a long black tail with a white tip

Where to find them:
shrubby areas with short trees and thick bushes, backyards and parks

Calls and songs:
calls "tow-hee" distinctly; also has a characteristic **call** that sounds like "drink-your-tea"

On the move:
short flights between shrubby areas and heavy **cover**; flashes white wing patches during flight

What they eat:
insects, seeds and fruit; comes to ground feeders

Nest:
cup; Mom constructs the nest

Eggs, chicks and childcare:
3–4 creamy-white eggs with brown marks; Mom incubates the eggs; Dad and Mom feed the young

Spends the winter:
in Florida, other southern states, Mexico, Central and South America

REAL QUICK

Size
7-8"

Nest
CUP

Feeder
GROUND

year-round

STAN'S COOL STUFF

The towhee is named for its distinctive "tow-hee" call. It hops backward with both feet, raking leaves to find insects and seeds. In southern coastal states, some have white eyes and others have red eyes. Only the white-eyed variety is found in Florida.

Brown-headed Cowbird

Look for the brown head

pg. 99

What to look for:
glossy black bird with a chocolate-brown head and a sharp, pointed gray bill

Where you'll find them:
forest edges, open fields, farmlands and backyards

Calls and songs:
sings a low, gurgling song that sounds like water moving; cowbird young are raised by other bird parents, but they still end up singing and calling like their own parents, whom they've never heard

On the move:
Mom flies quietly to another bird's nest, swiftly lays an egg, then flies quickly away

What they eat:
insects and seeds; visits seed feeders

Nest:
doesn't nest; lays eggs in the nests of other birds

Eggs, chicks and childcare:
5–7 white eggs with brown marks; the **host** bird incubates any number of cowbird eggs in her nest and feeds the cowbird young along with her own

Spends the winter:
in Florida and other southern states

REAL QUICK

Size
7½"

Nest
NONE

Feeder
TUBE OR HOPPER

year-round

SAW IT!

STAN'S COOL STUFF

Cowbirds are **brood parasites**, meaning they don't nest or raise their own families. Instead, they lay their eggs in other birds' nests, leaving the host birds to raise their young. Cowbirds have laid their eggs in the nests of more than 200 other bird species.

European Starling

Look for the glittering, iridescent feathers

What to look for:
shiny and **iridescent** purplish-black in spring and summer, speckled in fall and winter; yellow bill in spring, gray in fall; pointed wings and a short tail

Where you'll find them:
lines up with other starlings on power lines; found in all habitats but usually associated with people, farms, suburban yards and cities

Calls and songs:
mimics the songs of up to 20 bird species; mimics other sounds, even imitating the human voice

On the move:
large family groups gather with blackbirds in fall

What they eat:
bugs, seeds and fruit; visits seed and **suet** feeders

Nest:
cavity, filled with dried grass; often takes a cavity from other birds

Eggs, chicks and childcare:
4–6 bluish eggs with brown marks; Mom and Dad sit on the eggs and feed the babies

Spends the winter:
in Florida and other southern states

REAL QUICK

Size
7½"

Nest
CAVITY

Feeder
TUBE OR HOPPER

year-round

SAW IT!

STAN'S COOL STUFF

The starling is a mimic that can sound like any other bird. It's not a native bird; 100 starlings from Europe were introduced to New York City in 1890–91. Today, European Starlings are one of the most numerous songbirds in the country.

Red-winged Blackbird

Look for the red-and-yellow shoulder patches

What to look for:
black bird with red-and-yellow shoulder patches on upper wings; shoulder patches can be partially or completely covered up

Where you'll find them:
around marshes, wetlands, lakes and rivers

Calls and songs:
male sings and repeats calls from cattail tops and the surrounding **vegetation**

On the move:
flocks with as many as 10,000 birds gather in autumn, often with other blackbirds

What they eat:
seeds in spring and autumn, insects in summer; visits seed and **suet** feeders

Nest:
cup in a thick stand of cattails over shallow water

Eggs, chicks and childcare:
3–4 speckled bluish-green eggs; Mom does all the incubating, but both parents feed the babies

Spends the winter:
in Florida and other southern states, Mexico and Central America

REAL QUICK

Size
8½"

Nest
CUP

Feeder
TUBE OR HOPPER

year-round

SAW IT!

STAN'S COOL STUFF

During autumn and winter, thousands of these birds gather in farm fields, wetlands and marshes. Come spring, males sing to defend territories and show off their wing patches (**epaulets**) to the females. Later, males can be aggressive when defending their nests.

Common Grackle

Look for the shiny bluish-black head

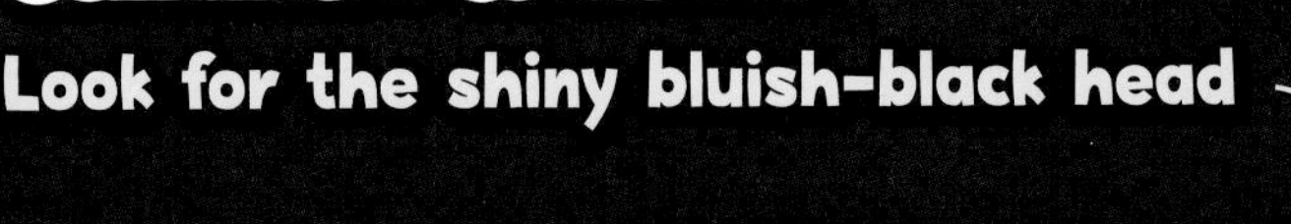

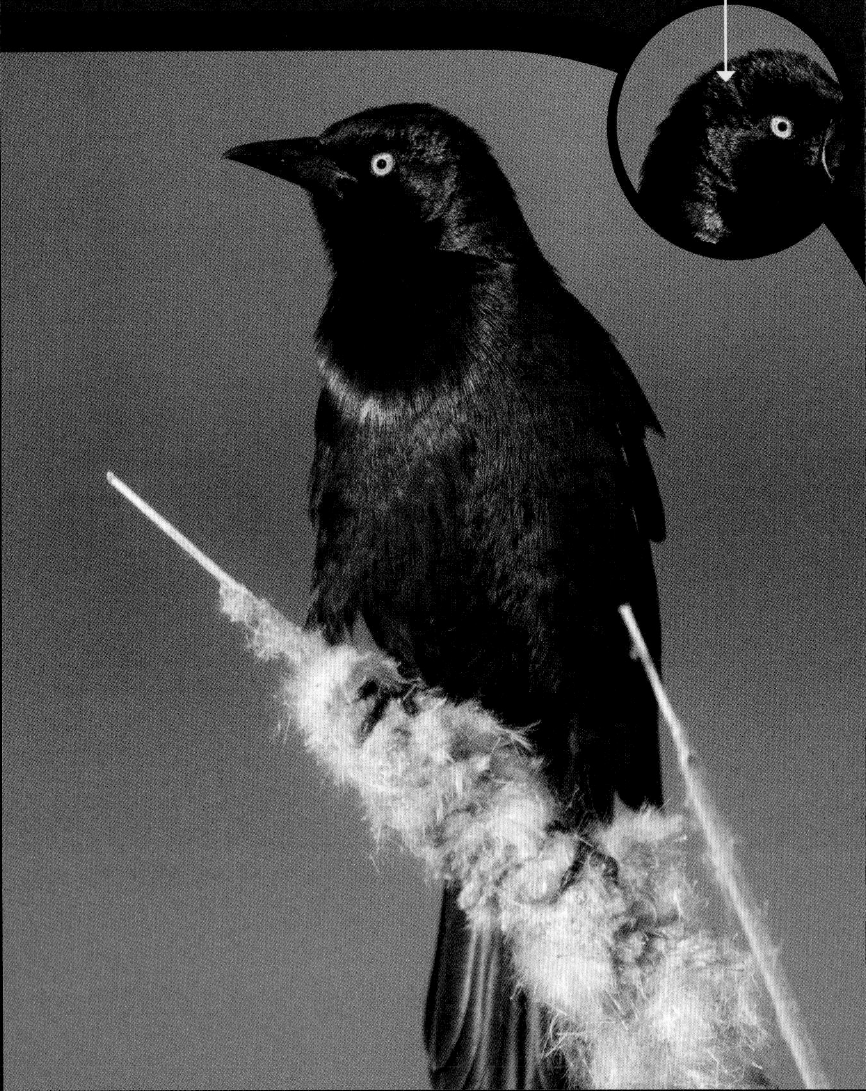

What to look for:
shiny bluish-black **iridescent** head, a purplish-brown body and super-bright golden eyes

Where you'll find them:
evergreen trees and shrubs, suburban and urban yards, open fields

Calls and songs:
gives a loud, raspy **call**

On the move:
travels in large flocks with other blackbirds; flight is usually level as opposed to an up-and-down pattern; male holds his tail in a deep V shape

What they eat:
fruit, seeds and bugs; visits seed and **suet** feeders

Nest:
cup, usually in a **colony** of up to 75 mated pairs

Eggs, chicks and childcare:
4–5 speckled greenish-white eggs; Mom sits on the eggs; Mom and Dad give food to the babies

Spends the winter:
in Florida and other southern states; moves around to find food

REAL QUICK

Size
11–13"

Nest
CUP

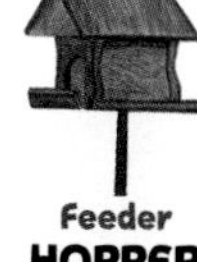

Feeder
HOPPER

year-round

SAW IT!

STAN'S COOL STUFF

The Common Grackle is a member of the blackbird family. Unlike most birds, it has stronger muscles to open its mouth. The muscles help it to pry apart crevices, where it finds bugs to eat. It's kind of like playing hide-and-seek for its food.

Common Gallinule

Look for the red bill with a yellow tip

What to look for:
nearly black overall with a yellow-tipped red bill, a red forehead and yellowish-green legs

Where you'll find them:
freshwater marshes and lakes

Calls and songs:
gives a series of fast, high-pitched clucks

On the move:
walks on floating **vegetation** or swims while on the hunt for bugs

What they eat:
insects, snails, seeds, green leaves, fruit and roots

Nest:
ground nest; Mom and Dad build it with cattails and other wetland plants

Eggs, chicks and childcare:
2–10 brown eggs with dark marks; Mom and Dad take turns incubating; young usually leave the nest within a few hours after hatching, but they stay with their family for a few months

Spends the winter:
in Florida and other southern states

REAL QUICK

Size
13–15"

Nest
GROUND

Feeder
NONE

year-round

SAW IT!

STAN'S COOL STUFF

This duck-like bird is also called the Pond Chicken. It was once known as the Common Moorhen. Females are known to lay some of their eggs in other gallinule nests. In the water, the young ride around on the backs of the adults.

American Coot

Look for the white bill

What to look for:
gray-to-black with a duck-like white bill, red eyes

Where you'll find them:
in large flocks on open water

Calls and songs:
a unique series of creaks, groans and clicks

On the move:
bobs head while swimming; takes off from water by scrambling across it with wings flapping; huge flocks of up to 1,000 birds gather for migration; migrates at night

What they eat:
insects and aquatic plants

Nest:
ground nest floating in water, anchored to plants

Eggs, chicks and childcare:
9–12 speckled pinkish-tan eggs; Mom and Dad sit on the eggs and feed the **hatchlings**

Spends the winter:
in Florida and other southern states, Mexico and Central America

REAL QUICK

Size
13–16"

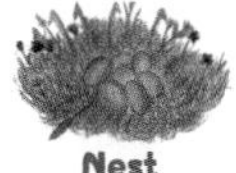

Nest
GROUND

Feeder
NONE

year-round

SAW IT!

STAN'S COOL STUFF

The coot is not a duck. Instead of webbed feet, it has large lobed toes! It's smaller than most other **waterfowl**, and it is a great diver and swimmer. You won't see it flying, but you may spot one trying to escape from a Bald Eagle (pg. 67). It's also called Mud Hen.

Boat-tailed Grackle

Look for the very long tail

MALE

FEMALE
pg. 123

What to look for:
glossy (**iridescent**) bluish-black bird with a very long tail and bright yellow eyes, or dark eyes

Where you'll find them:
coastal saltwater marshes and inland marshes

Calls and songs:
noisy, giving several harsh, high-pitched calls and several squeaks

On the move:
travels in large flocks with other blackbirds; flight is typically level, not in an up-and-down pattern

What they eat:
insects, berries, seeds, grains and fish; comes to seed and **suet** feeders

Nest:
cup; Mom makes it with mud or cow dung and grass; nests twice each year in a small **colony**

Eggs, chicks and childcare:
2–4 pale greenish-blue eggs with brown marks; Mom incubates the eggs and feeds the babies

Spends the winter:
doesn't **migrate**; stays in Florida year-round and moves around to find food

REAL QUICK

Size
15–17"

Nest
CUP

Feeder
HOPPER

year-round

SAW IT!

STAN'S COOL STUFF

Boat-tails are sometimes seen picking bugs off the backs of cattle. The birds north of Gainesville have yellow eyes; elsewhere in the state they have dark eyes. They're more common in Florida than the Common Grackle (pg. 27), although their range is smaller.

Fish Crow

Look for the small head

What to look for:
glossy black bird with a small head and black bill, a long black tail and black feet

Where you'll find them:
all habitats—coastlines, rivers, lakes, wetlands, wilderness, rural, suburban, cities

Calls and songs:
gives a high-pitched, nasal "cah" **call**; imitates other birds and people

On the move:
gathers in winter flocks of up to 100 birds

What they eat:
insects, dead carcasses (**carrion**), clams, mussels, snails, slugs and other **mollusks**, berries and seeds; comes to seed and **suet** feeders

Nest:
platform, often builds a stick nest in a palm tree; nests in a small **colony**

Eggs, chicks and childcare:
4–5 speckled blue or grayish-green eggs; Mom and Dad sit on the eggs and feed the young

Spends the winter:
doesn't **migrate**; stays in Florida year-round

REAL QUICK

Size
16"

Nest
PLATFORM

Feeder
HOPPER

year-round

SAW IT!

STAN'S COOL STUFF

This crow is mainly a bird of the coast and major rivers, but it's all over Florida. It breaks open mollusk shells by dropping them onto rocks from above. You can identify it by its call. It is higher in pitch than the call of the American Crow (pg. 37).

American Crow

Look for the glossy black feathers

What to look for:
glossy black all over and a black bill

Where you'll find them:
all habitats—wilderness, rural, suburban, cities

Calls and songs:
a harsh "caw" **call**; imitates other birds and people

On the move:
flaps constantly and glides downward; moves around to find food; gathers in huge communal flocks of more than 10,000 birds during winter

What they eat:
fruit, insects, mammals, fish and dead carcasses (**carrion**); visits seed and **suet** feeders

Nest:
platform; often uses the same site every year if a Great Horned Owl (pg. 141) hasn't taken it

Eggs, chicks and childcare:
4–6 speckled bluish-to-olive eggs; Mom sits on the eggs; Mom and Dad feed the youngsters

Spends the winter:
in Florida

REAL QUICK

Size
18"

Nest
PLATFORM

Feeder
HOPPER

year-round

SAW IT!

STAN'S COOL STUFF

The crow is one of the smartest of all birds. It's very social and often entertains itself by chasing other birds. It eats roadkill but avoids being hit by vehicles. Some can live as long as 20 years! Crows without mates, called helpers, help to raise the young.

Black Vulture

Look for the naked dark gray head

What to look for:
naked dark gray head and legs, an ivory bill and a short tail; appears black in flight with light gray wing tips

Where you'll find them:
in trees, sunning itself with wings outstretched, drying after a rain

Calls and songs:
mostly **mute**, just grunts and groans

On the move:
holds wings straight out to the sides during flight

What they eat:
dead carcasses (**carrion**); may capture small live mammals; parents **regurgitate** food for the young

Nest:
no nest, or on a stump or the ground; may use an empty nest; often nests with other Black Vultures

Eggs, chicks and childcare:
1–3 light green eggs with dark marks; Mom and Dad do the **incubation** and feed the babies

Spends the winter:
doesn't **migrate**; stays in Florida year-round

REAL QUICK

Size
25-28"

Nest
NONE

Feeder
NONE

year-round

SAW IT!

STAN'S COOL STUFF

People also call this bird the Black Buzzard. It's not as good at finding carrion as the Turkey Vulture (pg. 41), so its sense of smell may be weaker. If startled, especially at the nest, it regurgitates with power and accuracy. Families stay together for up to a year.

Turkey Vulture

Look for the naked red head

What to look for:
naked red head and legs and an ivory bill; juvenile has a gray-to-blackish head and bill

Where you'll find them:
in trees, sunning itself with wings outstretched, drying after a rain

Calls and songs:
mostly **mute**, just grunts and groans

On the move:
holds wings in an upright V in flight, teetering from wing tip to wing tip as it soars and hovers

What they eat:
dead carcasses (**carrion**); parents **regurgitate** food for their young

Nest:
no nest, or in a minimal nest on a cliff, in a cave, or even sometimes in a hollow tree trunk

Eggs, chicks and childcare:
1–3 white eggs with brown marks; Mom and Dad incubate the eggs and feed the baby vultures

Spends the winter:
in Florida, other southern states, Mexico, Central and South America

REAL QUICK

Size
26–32"

Nest
NONE

Feeder
NONE

year-round

SAW IT!

STAN'S COOL STUFF

This is one of the few birds with a good sense of smell. It has a strong bill for tearing apart flesh. Unlike hawks and eagles, it has weak feet more suited for walking than grasping wiggly **prey**. The bare head reduces its risk of getting diseases from carcasses.

Double-crested Cormorant

Look for the large, hooked bill

What to look for:
large black waterbird with unusual blue eyes, a long snake-like neck, and large gray bill with a yellow base and hooked tip

Where you'll find them:
usually roosts in large groups in trees near water

Calls and songs:
grunts, pops and groans—none are pleasant sounds at all!

On the move:
swims underwater to catch fish, holding its wings at its sides; flies in a large V-shaped formation or a straight line

What they eat:
small fish and aquatic insects

Nest:
platform near or over open water, in a **colony**

Eggs, chicks and childcare:
3–4 bluish-white eggs; parents take turns sitting on the eggs and feeding the young

Spends the winter:
in Florida and other southern states, Mexico and Central America

REAL QUICK

Size
31–35"

Nest
PLATFORM

Feeder
NONE

year-round
migration

SAW IT!

STAN'S COOL STUFF

The cormorant lacks the oil gland that other birds have, which keeps feathers from getting waterlogged. To dry out, it faces the sun and poses with outstretched wings. "Double-crested" refers to the two unusual crests on its head, but these aren't often seen.

Anhinga

Look for the long, thin neck

What to look for:
black with glossy green-and-white streaks and spots on the wings, a long neck and tail, and a long, thin yellow bill; female has a light brown neck and chest; juvenile has a light brown-to-white body

Where you'll find them:
freshwater habitats

Calls and songs:
usually silent; occasionally gives a creaking or croaking **call**

On the move:
dives and maneuvers well underwater; a strong flier, often soaring like a bird of prey

What they eat:
fish, aquatic insects, **crustaceans**, small mammals

Nest:
platform; Mom and Dad construct it

Eggs, chicks and childcare:
2–4 light blue eggs; Mom and Dad alternate sitting on the eggs and feeding the babies

Spends the winter:
doesn't **migrate** in Florida; stays here all year

REAL QUICK

Size
33-37"

Nest
PLATFORM

Feeder
NONE

year-round

SAW IT!

STAN'S COOL STUFF

This bird is also called Snakebird. After diving into the water, it surfaces with just its head and neck showing, like a snake. To catch fish, it skewers them with its long, sharp bill. It often strikes a pose, spreading its waterlogged wings to dry in the sun.

Downy Woodpecker

Look for the small, short bill

What to look for:
spotted wings, white belly, red mark on the back of the head and a small, short bill; female lacks a red mark on the head

Where you'll find them:
wherever trees are present

Calls and songs:
repeats a high-pitched "peek-peek" **call**; drums on trees or logs with its bill to announce its territory

On the move:
flies in an up-and-down pattern; makes short flights from tree to tree

What they eat:
insects and seeds; visits **suet** and seed feeders

Nest:
cavity in a dead tree; digs out a perfectly round entrance hole; the bottom of the cavity is wider than the top, and it's lined with fallen woodchips

Eggs, chicks and childcare:
3–5 white eggs; Mom incubates the eggs; both parents take care of the kiddies

Spends the winter:
doesn't **migrate**; stays in Florida year-round

REAL QUICK

Size
6"

Nest
CAVITY

Feeder
SUET

year-round

SAW IT!

STAN'S COOL STUFF

The Downy is abundant and widespread where trees are present. Like other woodpeckers, it pulls insects from tiny places with its long, barbed tongue. It has stiff tail feathers, which help to support it as it clings to trees. During winter, it will roost in a cavity.

Yellow-bellied Sapsucker

Look for the red chin

What to look for:
checkered back, yellow chest and belly, and a red forehead, crown and chin; female has a white chin

Where you'll find them:
small woods, forests, suburban and rural areas, small to medium trees that have rows of sap holes

Calls and songs:
quiet with few vocalizations but will meow like a cat; drums on hollow tree branches irregularly (not in a regular pattern, like other woodpeckers)

On the move:
short up-and-down flights with rapid wingbeats

What they eat:
insects, nutritious sap in trees; visits **suet** feeders

Nest:
cavity that Mom and Dad **excavate**, often in a live tree—but a dead tree will work, too!

Eggs, chicks and childcare:
5–6 white eggs; Mom and Dad incubate the eggs and feed the **brood**

Spends the winter:
in Florida and other southern states, Mexico and Central America

REAL QUICK

Size
8–9"

Nest
CAVITY

Feeder
SUET

winter

SAW IT!

STAN'S COOL STUFF

Sapsuckers are woodpeckers that drill rows of holes in trees to get to the sap. **Tree sap** is full of nutrients and minerals. Sapsuckers don't actually suck the sap out of the holes; rather, they lap it with their long, bristly tongues. Oozing sap also attracts bugs to eat.

Hairy Woodpecker

Look for the large bill

What to look for:
spotted wings, white belly, large bill and red mark on the back of the head; female lacks a red mark

Where you'll find them:
forests and wooded backyards, parks

Calls and songs:
a sharp chirp before landing on feeders; drums on hollow logs, branches or stovepipes in spring

On the move:
short up-and-down flights from tree to tree with rapid wingbeats

What they eat:
insects, nuts, seeds; visits **suet** and seed feeders

Nest:
cavity; prefers a live tree; excavates a larger, more oval entry than the round hole of the Downy Woodpecker (pg. 47); usually excavates under a branch, which helps to shield the entrance

Eggs, chicks and childcare:
3–6 white eggs; parents sit on the eggs and bring food to feed their babies

Spends the winter:
doesn't **migrate**; stays in Florida year-round

REAL QUICK

Size
9"

Nest
CAVITY

Feeder
SUET

year-round

SAW IT!

STAN'S COOL STUFF

The Hairy is nearly identical to the Downy Woodpecker, but it's larger and has a larger, longer bill. It has a barbed tongue, which it uses to pull out bugs from trees. At the base of its bill, tiny bristle-like feathers protect its nostrils from excavated wood dust.

Red-bellied Woodpecker

Look for the black-and-white striped back

What to look for:

zebra-striped back, white rump, red crown and red nape of neck; female has a light gray crown

Where you'll find them:

shady woodlands, forest edges and backyards

Calls and songs:

calls a loud "querrr" and a low "chug-chug-chug"

On the move:

rapid wingbeats in flight, going up and down like a roller coaster

What they eat:

beetles and other insects, spiders, centipedes, nuts and fruit; visits **suet** and seed feeders

Nest:

cavity in a dead tree; excavates a new hole in last year's tree below the previous cavity

Eggs, chicks and childcare:

4–5 white eggs; Mom incubates the eggs during the day and Dad takes night duty; both parents feed the baby woodpeckers

Spends the winter:

doesn't **migrate**; stays in Florida year-round and moves around to find food

REAL QUICK

Size
9–9½"

Nest
CAVITY

Feeder
SUET

year-round

SAW IT!

STAN'S COOL STUFF

This bird is named for its faint pink belly patch. It excavates dead wood to find bugs to eat, and hammers acorns and berries into cracks in trees to store for winter food. The population and range of this woodpecker are increasing across the country.

Ruddy Turnstone

Look for the black-and-white head

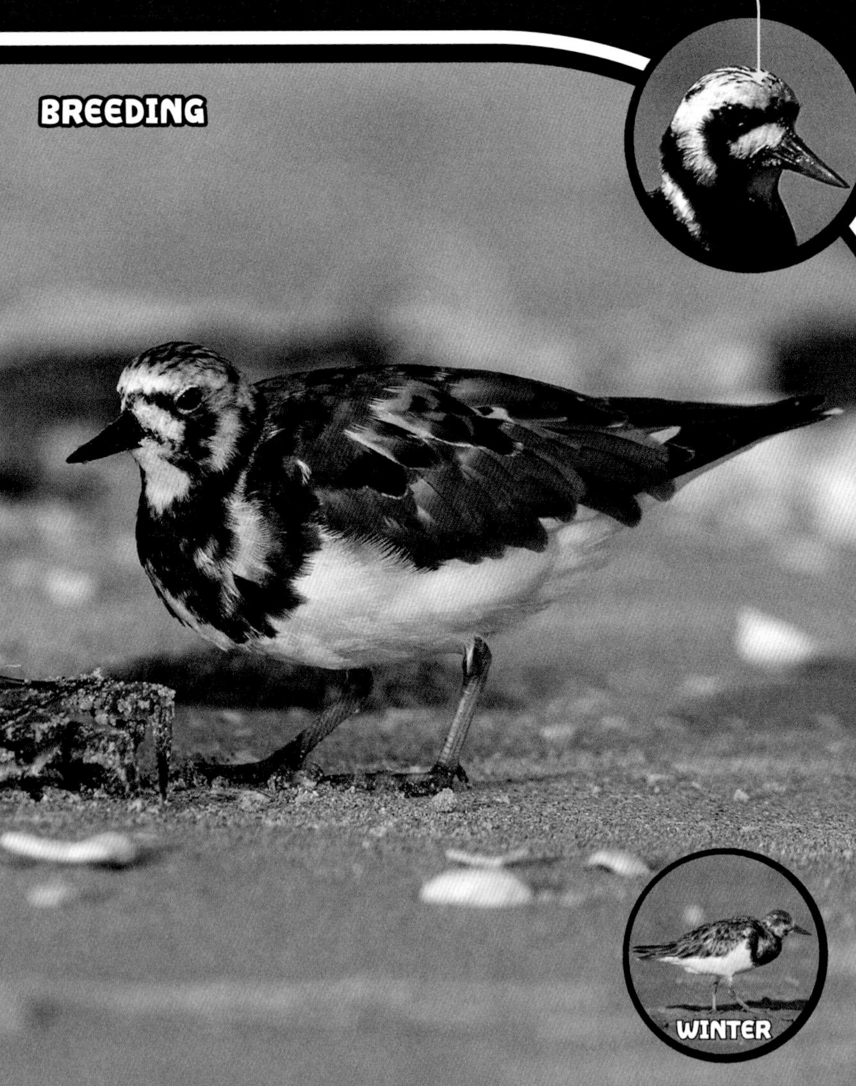

What to look for:
unusual black-and-white head pattern, black bib, white throat and belly, black-and-rust wings and back, slightly upturned black bill; winter **plumage** has a brown-and-white head and chest pattern

Where you'll find them:
rocky beaches, sandy beaches, crabbing operations (where it eats scraps from nets)

Calls and songs:
if stressed, gives a fast, high-pitched alarm **call**

On the move:
turns over stones on rocky beaches to find food

What they eat:
aquatic insects, fish, snails and other **mollusks**, crabs and other **crustaceans**, worms, bird eggs

Nest:
ground nest; just Mom builds it

Eggs, chicks and childcare:
3–4 speckled olive eggs; Dad and Mom sit on the eggs; Mom leaves before the babies leave the nest (**fledge**), so Dad feeds the babies by himself

Spends the winter:
in coastal Florida and other Gulf Coast states

REAL QUICK

Size
9½"

Nest
GROUND

Feeder
NONE

migration
winter

SAW IT!

STAN'S COOL STUFF

This bird is named for its behavior of turning over stones to find food. Also called Rock Plover, it can be very tolerant of people when it feeds. The male develops a bare spot on his belly (brood patch) to warm the young, something only females normally have.

Black-bellied Plover

Look for the black belly

BREEDING

WINTER
pg. 169

What to look for:
striking black-and-white bird with a black face, chest, belly, legs and bill, and a white cap, nape of neck and lower belly near the tail

Where you'll find them:
at the beach

Calls and songs:
calls a single high-pitched, slurred "fee-a-wee"

On the move:
often darts across the ground to grab a bug and run off with it; male performs a butterfly-like courtship flight to attract females

What they eat:
insects, worms, clams and **crustaceans**

Nest:
ground nest; Dad and Mom construct it together

Eggs, chicks and childcare:
3–4 pinkish or greenish eggs with blackish-brown marks; parents incubate the eggs; Dad feeds the kids, who quickly learn how to feed themselves

Spends the winter:
along coastal Florida

REAL QUICK

Size
11–12"

Nest
GROUND

Feeder
NONE

migration
winter

SAW IT!

STAN'S COOL STUFF

The fall migrators start arriving in Florida in July and August. During flight, this bird displays a white rump and a white stripe on its wings. It starts breeding at 3 years of age. The female leaves her mate and their young about 12 days after the eggs hatch.

Ring-necked Duck

Look for the white rings on the blue bill

pg. 131

What to look for:
handsome duck with a black head, chest and back, light gray-to-whitish sides, a blue bill with a thick white ring near the tip and a thinner white ring at the base; head is tall with a sloping forehead

Where you'll find them:
usually in larger freshwater lakes rather than saltwater marshes

Calls and songs:
male gives a quick series of grating barks and grunts; female gives high-pitched peeps

On the move:
dives underwater to forage for food; takes to flight by springing up off the water

What they eat:
aquatic plants and insects

Nest:
ground nest; Mom builds it

Eggs, chicks and childcare:
8–10 grayish-to-brown eggs; Mom incubates the eggs and teaches the young how to feed

Spends the winter:
in Florida and other southern states

REAL QUICK

Size
16–18"

Nest
GROUND

Feeder
NONE

winter

SAW IT!

STAN'S COOL STUFF

The Ring-necked Duck is one of the most abundant winter ducks in Florida. It's also called the Ring-billed Duck due to the obvious ring on its bill. Oddly enough, it was named for the faint rusty collar on its neck, which is nearly impossible to see.

American Oystercatcher

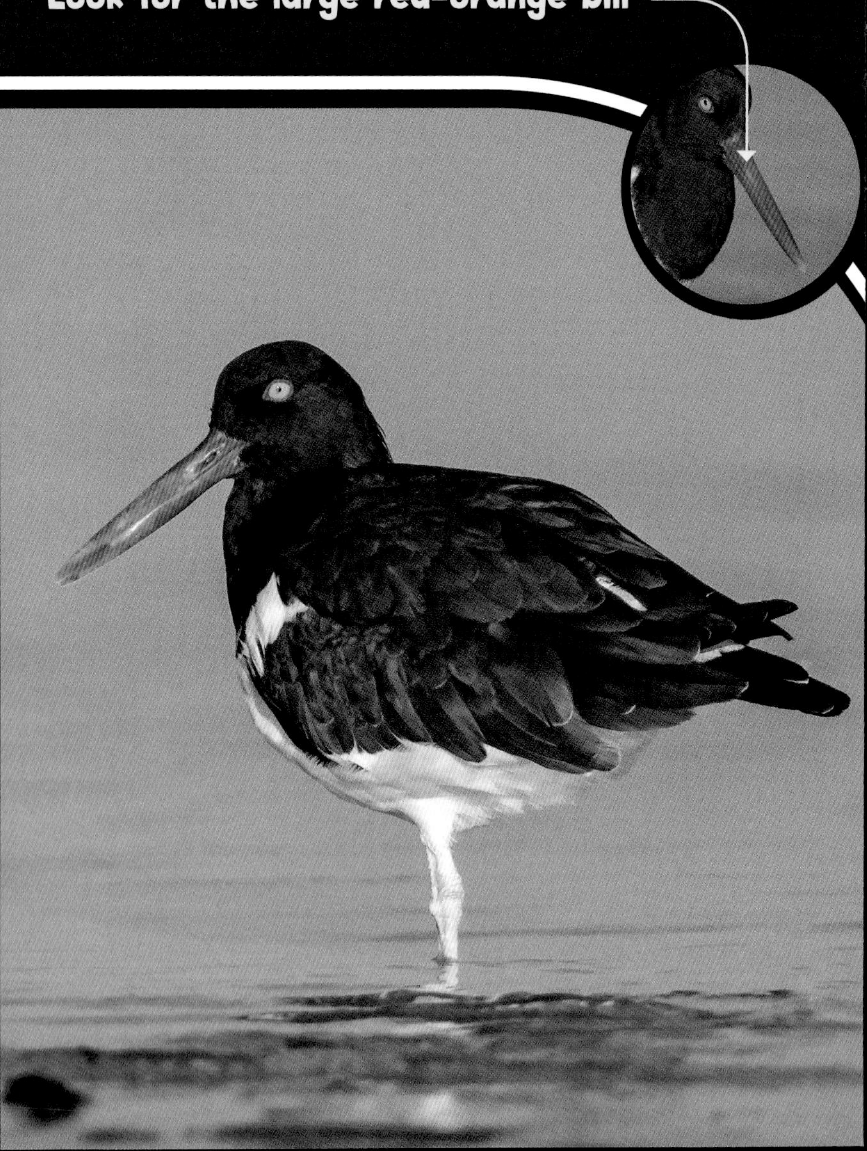
Look for the large red-orange bill

What to look for:
chunky shorebird with a large red-orange bill and a red eye-ring, black head, a white chest and belly, dark brown wings, sides and back, and pink legs

Where you'll find them:
at the beach

Calls and songs:
gives a series of loud, high-pitched calls that sound like "wheep"

On the move:
stabs its bill between the shells of oysters, clams and other **mollusks** to prevent them from closing, or hammers shells, shattering them with a few powerful blows

What they eat:
mollusks, **crustaceans**, shellfish and worms

Nest:
ground nest; Dad and Mom construct it

Eggs, chicks and childcare:
2–4 olive eggs with brown marks; Dad and Mom take turns incubating and doing the childcare

Spends the winter:
along coastal Florida

REAL QUICK

Size
18–19"

Nest
GROUND

Feeder
NONE

year-round

SAW IT!

STAN'S COOL STUFF

This large, handsome shorebird stands out at the beach. It uses its heavy, flattened bill to pry open shellfish and probe the sand for mollusks. The young quickly learn the oyster-opening technique from their parents and are soon feeding themselves.

Pileated Woodpecker

Look for the bright red crest

What to look for:

bright red crest that looks like a hat; bright red forehead and mustache, and a black back; female has a black forehead and lacks a red mustache

Where you'll find them:

prefers areas with lots of woodland

Calls and songs:

drums on hollow branches, chimneys and such to announce territory; loud, rapid "cuk-cuk-cuk" calls carry over a long distance

On the move:

white leading edge of wings flashes brightly during flight

What they eat:

insects (especially its favorite, carpenter ants); visits **suet** feeders and feeders with peanuts

Nest:

cavity in a dead or live tree trunk

Eggs, chicks and childcare:

3–5 white eggs; Mom and Dad sit on the eggs and regurgitate bugs to feed the youngsters

Spends the winter:

doesn't **migrate**; stays in Florida year-round

REAL QUICK

Size
19"

Nest
CAVITY

Feeder
SUET

year-round

SAW IT!

STAN'S COOL STUFF

This is our largest woodpecker. It's shy, despite its size. It digs oval holes up to a few feet long in tree trunks, looking for bugs to eat. You'll see large wood chips at the base of those trees. The young come out of the nest looking and sounding just like the adults.

Osprey

Look for the dark line through the eyes

What to look for:
white chest, belly and head, with a dark eye line

Where you'll find them:
always near water, from rivers to wetlands

Calls and songs:
a high-pitched, whistle-like **call**, often given in flight as a warning

On the move:
can hover for a few seconds before diving to catch a fish; carries fish in a head-first position in flight for better aerodynamics

What they eat:
fish

Nest:
platform made with twigs; on a raised wooden platform, man-made tower or in a tall dead tree

Eggs, chicks and childcare:
2–4 white eggs with brown marks; parents sit on the eggs and feed the **hatchlings**

Spends the winter:
some **migrate** into Florida, other southern states, Mexico, and Central and South America; others live in Florida year-round and do not leave

REAL QUICK

Size
21–24"

Nest
PLATFORM

Feeder
NONE

year-round

SAW IT!

STAN'S COOL STUFF

The Osprey is only species in its family. It is the only **raptor** that plunges feet first into the water to catch fish. Bald Eagles (pg. 67) will harass it for its catch. At one time, it was almost extinct. It was introduced to many regions, and populations are now stable.

Bald Eagle

Look for the white head

What to look for:
white head and tail, curved yellow bill and yellow feet; juvenile has white speckles and a gray bill

Where you'll find them:
often near water; likes open areas with daily food

Calls and songs:
weak, high-pitched screams, one after another

On the move:
a spectacular aerial mating **display**: one eagle flips upside down and locks talons with another; both fall, tumbling to earth, then break apart and fly off

What they eat:
fish, **carrion** (dead rabbits and squirrels), birds (mainly ducks), prefers American Coots (pg. 31)

Nest:
massive platform of sticks, usually in a tree; nests used for many years can weigh up to 1,000 pounds

Eggs, chicks and childcare:
2–3 off-white eggs; Mom and Dad share all duties

Spends the winter:
some **migrate** into Florida and other southern states; others live in Florida year-round and do not leave

REAL QUICK

Size
31–37"

Nest
PLATFORM

Feeder
NONE

year-round
migration

SAW IT!

STAN'S COOL STUFF

Bald Eagles nearly became extinct, but they're doing well now. Their wingspan is huge, stretching out to 7½ feet! They return to the same nest and add more sticks each year, enlarging it over time. The heads and tails of juveniles turn white at 4–5 years.

Wood Stork

Look for the bald, mostly dark head

What to look for:
white body with a bald, mostly dark head and a large, thick, down-curved bill; black legs, pink feet, and a black tail and wing tips, seen in flight

Where you'll find them:
wetlands

Calls and songs:
usually silent, but **nestlings** are very loud, making nasal-sounding calls over and over

On the move:
shuffles its feet to stir up fish to catch; swings its open bill through the water until it contacts **prey**, then snaps the bill shut

What they eat:
fish, amphibians, snakes, large aquatic bugs, snails

Nest:
platform, in a large **colony**, often high up in a tree

Eggs, chicks and childcare:
2–4 white eggs; parents take turns sitting on the eggs and feeding the baby storks

Spends the winter:
many don't **migrate**; stays in Florida

REAL QUICK

Size
42–44"

Nest
PLATFORM

Feeder
NONE

year-round
summer

SAW IT!

STAN'S COOL STUFF

The stork is on state and federal endangered species lists. Like many wading birds, it has less than 20 percent of the population than it had a century ago. It will abandon its eggs or young when food is scarce. It often will not breed until it's 4–5 years old.

Indigo Bunting

Look for the vibrant blue feathers

What to look for:
vibrant blue with scattered dark marks on the wings and tail; **plumage** gleams in direct sunlight and appears dull on cloudy days or in shade

Where you'll find them:
woodland edges, where it feasts on insects; parks and yards

Calls and songs:
male often sings from treetops to attract a mate; female is quiet

On the move:
migrates at night in flocks of 5–10 birds

What they eat:
insects, seeds and fruit; only visits seed feeders early in spring, when bugs are in short supply

Nest:
cup in a small tree or shrub, low to the ground

Eggs, chicks and childcare:
3–4 pale blue eggs; Mom sits on the eggs and attends to the young

Spends the winter:
migrates to southern Florida, Mexico, Central and South America

REAL QUICK

Size
5½"

Nest
CUP

Feeder
HOPPER

summer
migration
winter

SAW IT!

STAN'S COOL STUFF

This male is actually gray! Like Blue Jays (pg. 79) and other blue birds, there's no blue pigment in the feathers. Sunlight **refraction** in the structure of the feathers makes them look blue. Males **molt** in autumn and look like the brown females during winter.

Tree Swallow

Look for the white chin and chest

What to look for:
blue-green bird with a white chin, chest and belly, and long, pointed wings

Where you'll find them:
ponds, lakes, rivers and farm fields

Calls and songs:
gives a series of gurgles and chirps; chatters when upset or threatened

On the move:
flies back and forth across fields, feeding on bugs; uses rapid wingbeats, and then glides; family units gather in large flocks for migration

What they eat:
insects—big and small

Nest:
cavity; adds grass and lines it with feathers; uses an old woodpecker hole or a wooden nest box

Eggs, chicks and childcare:
4–6 white eggs; Mom sits on the eggs; Mom and Dad bring bugs to feed the babies

Spends the winter:
in Florida, Mexico and Central America

REAL QUICK

Size
5-6"

Nest
CAVITY

Feeder
NONE

year-round
migration

SAW IT!

STAN'S COOL STUFF

The swallow is a good bird to have around because it eats many bugs. You can attract it with a nest box, but it will compete with Eastern Bluebirds (pg. 75) for the cavity. It finds dropped feathers to line its nest and plays with them on its way back to the nest.

Eastern Bluebird

Look for the rusty-red chest

MALE

What to look for:
sky-blue head, back, wings and tail, with a rusty-red chest and white belly; female is grayer

Where you'll find them:
open habitats (prefers farm fields, pastures and roadsides), forest edges, parks and yards

Calls and songs:
male repeats a distinctive "chur-lee chur chur-lee" song mostly in spring as he displays to the female

On the move:
short flights from tree to tree; often perches in trees or on posts, dropping to ground to grab bugs

What they eat:
insects, fruit; visits mealworm and **suet** feeders

Nest:
cavity; adds a soft lining in an old woodpecker hole or a bluebird nest box

Eggs, chicks and childcare:
4–5 pale blue eggs; Mom incubates the eggs, and Dad and Mom feed the kids; 2 broods per year

Spends the winter:
in Florida and other southern states; moves just far enough south to avoid harsh winter weather

REAL QUICK

Size
7"

Nest
CAVITY

Feeder
MEALWORM

year-round

SAW IT!

STAN'S COOL STUFF

The bluebird is a cousin of the American Robin (pg. 165). It was nearly eliminated due to a lack of tree cavities, but it's thriving now thanks to people who have put up bluebird nest boxes. The young of the first **brood** sometimes help care for the second brood.

Florida Scrub-Jay

Look for the light blue head

What to look for:
dark blue body with a lighter blue head, white forehead and whitish belly, and a very long tail

Where you'll find them:
scrubby **habitat**, usually around oak trees that are about 10 feet tall; not a backyard bird, like the Blue Jay (pg. 79)

Calls and songs:
gives a wide variety of raspy, hoarse calls

On the move:
carries seeds in flight in a pouch under its tongue

What they eat:
insects, fruit and seeds; comes to seed feeders

Nest:
cup of twigs in a tree, near the main trunk

Eggs, chicks and childcare:
3–6 pale green eggs with dark marks; Mom sits on the eggs, but Mom and Dad feed the babies

Spends the winter:
doesn't **migrate**; stays in Florida year-round

REAL QUICK

Size
11"

Nest
CUP

Feeder
HOPPER

year-round

SAW IT!

STAN'S COOL STUFF

This bird is a threatened species, found in central Florida and nowhere else. It's had a 90 percent decline in population due to habitat loss during the last century. Young scrub-jays from one year help their parents to raise the babies of the next year.

Blue Jay

Look for the large crest

What to look for:
vivid blue bird with a black **necklace**; a large crest, which the jay raises and lowers at will

Where you'll find them:
in the woods and all around your backyard

Calls and songs:
loud, noisy and mimics other birds; screams like a hawk around feeders to scare away other birds

On the move:
carries seeds and nuts in a pouch under its tongue during flight

What they eat:
insects, fruit, seeds, nuts, bird eggs and babies in other nests; visits seed feeders, ground feeders with corn and any feeder with peanuts

Nest:
cup of twigs in a tree, near the main trunk

Eggs, chicks and childcare:
4–5 speckled green-to-blue eggs; Mom sits on the eggs; Mom and Dad feed the little ones

Spends the winter:
in Florida; moves around to find an abundant source of food

REAL QUICK

Size
12"

Nest
CUP

Feeder
HOPPER

year-round

SAW IT!

STAN'S COOL STUFF

Blue Jays are very intelligent. They store food in hiding places, called caches, to eat later. They can remember where they hide thousands of nuts! Jays are known as the alarm of the forest, screaming at intruders in the woods.

Belted Kingfisher

Look for the large, ragged crest

What to look for:
broad blue band on a white chest, ragged crest; female has a rusty band below her blue band

Where you'll find them:
rarely away from water; usually at banks of rivers, lakes and large streams

Calls and songs:
gives a loud **call** that sounds like a machine gun rattling; mates know each other's call

On the move:
flashes the small white patches on its dark wing tips during flight

What they eat:
small fish

Nest:
cavity in the bank of a river, lake or cliff; digs a tunnel up to 4 feet long to the nest chamber

Eggs, chicks and childcare:
6–7 white eggs; Mom and Dad sit on the eggs and feed fish to their youngsters

Spends the winter:
in Florida, other southern states, Mexico, Central and South America

REAL QUICK

Size
12–14"

Nest
CAVITY

Feeder
NONE

year-round
winter

SAW IT!

STAN'S COOL STUFF

Belted Kingfishers perch near water and dive in headfirst to catch fish. Parents drop dead fish into the water to teach their young to dive. Kingfishers have short legs with two toes fused together. This helps a lot when they dig (**excavate**) a burrow for nesting.

Little Blue Heron

Look for the black-tipped blue-gray bill

BREEDING

MOLTING JUVENILE

WHITE JUVENILE

NON-BREEDING

What to look for:
dark blue-to-purple heron with a reddish-purple head and neck, several long plumes on the crown, dull green legs and feet, and a blue-gray bill with a black tip during breeding season; non-breeding bill is gray; juvenile is white with yellowish legs and feet, and a gray bill with a black tip

Where you'll find them:
look for it feeding in freshwater lakes, rivers and ponds, and in saltwater marshes and wetlands

Calls and songs:
often silent but gives a deep, hoarse **call** if startled

On the move:
stalks **prey** slowly

What they eat:
fish and aquatic insects

Nest:
platform, in a large **colony** near saltwater sites

Eggs, chicks and childcare:
2–6 light blue eggs; parents share the childcare

Spends the winter:
many don't **migrate**, staying in Florida all year; northern birds join the residents during winter

REAL QUICK

Size
22-26"

Nest
PLATFORM

Feeder
NONE

year-round
summer

SAW IT!

STAN'S COOL STUFF

This heron is unusual because the young look very different from the adults. They start out with all-white feathers, which makes them look like Snowy Egrets (pg. 207). During the first year they turn blotchy white. By the second year they look like the adults.

Tricolored Heron

Look for a blue-and-white neck

BREEDING

NON-BREEDING

What to look for:
blue-gray head, neck and wings, white on the neck and belly, yellow-to-green legs, and a long blue bill with a dark tip during breeding season; non-breeding bill is gray

Where you'll find them:
wetland habitats; usually in saltwater marshes but also in freshwater marshes inland

Calls and songs:
gives a raspy nasal **call** if startled, then flies off

On the move:
hunts by standing still and waiting, but it will also chase after small fish

What they eat:
fish and aquatic insects

Nest:
platform, in a **colony** with other herons; one adult is always on duty at the nest

Eggs, chicks and childcare:
3–6 light blue eggs; Mom and Dad share the jobs of incubating and feeding the babies

Spends the winter:
many don't **migrate** and don't leave Florida

REAL QUICK

Size
24–28"

Nest
PLATFORM

Feeder
NONE

year-round
summer

SAW IT!

STAN'S COOL STUFF

The Tricolored can be identified by its white undersides. Unlike other herons, it wasn't hunted for its plumes. But its numbers still declined due to the loss of wetland habitats. In Florida, it's less numerous during summer. It's known to wander as far as Kansas.

Look for the heavily streaked chest

FEMALE

MALE
pg. 195

What to look for:
brown bird with heavy streaks on a white chest

Where you'll find them:
forests, city and suburban areas, around homes, parks and farms

Calls and songs:
male sings a loud, cheerful warbling song

On the move:
moves around in small family units; never travels long distances

What they eat:
seeds, fruit and leaf buds; comes to seed feeders and feeders with a glop of grape jelly

Nest:
cup, but occasionally in a cavity; likes to nest in a hanging flower basket or on a front door wreath

Eggs, chicks and childcare:
4–5 pale blue eggs, lightly marked; Mom sits on the eggs and Dad feeds her while she incubates; Mom and Dad feed the **brood**

Spends the winter:
in most of Florida; moves around to find food

REAL QUICK

Size
5"

Nest
CUP

Feeder
TUBE OR HOPPER

year-round

SAW IT!

STAN'S COOL STUFF

The House Finch is very social and can be a common bird at feeders. It was introduced to New York from the western U.S. in the 1940s. Now it's found all across the country. Unfortunately, it suffers from a fatal eye disease that causes the eyes to crust over.

House Wren

Look for the slightly curved bill

What to look for:
brown bird with light brown marks on the wings and tail, a slightly curved brown bill

Where you'll find them:
brushy yards, woodlands, forest edges and parks

Calls and songs:
sings a lot; during the mating season, it sings from dawn to dusk

On the move:
short flights from protective bushes; holds its tail up briefly after landing

What they eat:
insects, spiders and snails

Nest:
cavity in a tree or birdhouse; easily attracted to a nest box; builds a twiggy nest in spring and lines it with pine needles and grass

Eggs, chicks and childcare:
4–6 tan eggs with brown marks; Mom and Dad incubate the eggs and raise the chicks

Spends the winter:
in Florida, other southern states and Mexico

REAL QUICK

Size
5"

Nest
CAVITY

Feeder
NONE

winter

SAW IT!

STAN'S COOL STUFF

The male chooses several nest cavities and puts a few small twigs in each. The female selects one cavity, and then fills it with short twigs. Often she will have trouble fitting long twigs through the entrance hole, but she'll try again and again until she's successful.

Carolina Wren

Look for the bold white eyebrows

What to look for:
orange-yellow chest and belly, a white throat, bold white eyebrows, and a stubby tail, often held up

Where to find them:
brushy yards and woodlands

Calls and songs:
sings year-round; male sings up to 40 song types, singing one song repeatedly before switching to another; female also sings, resulting in duets

On the move:
short, fast flights, often perching high up to sing before flying again

What they eat:
insects, fruit and few seeds; comes to **suet** and mealworm feeders

Nest:
cavity; nests in birdhouses and in unusual places, like mailboxes, car bumpers and broken taillights

Eggs, chicks and childcare:
4–6 white (sometimes pink) eggs with brown marks; Mom incubates; parents feed the babies

Spends the winter:
doesn't **migrate**; stays in Florida year-round

REAL QUICK

Size
5½"

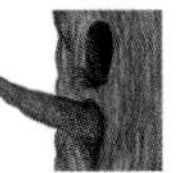

Nest
CAVITY

Feeder
SUET OR MEALWORM

year-round

SAW IT!

STAN'S COOL STUFF

Carolina Wrens have a long-term **pair bond**. Mated pairs stay with each other in their territory all year long. They can have up to three broods per year. The male often takes over feeding the young when the female nests again.

Indigo Bunting

Look for the faint blue on the wings

pg. 71

What to look for:
light brown bird with faint wing bars and faint blue on the wings

Where you'll find them:
woodland edges, where it feasts on insects; parks and yards

Calls and songs:
female is quiet; male often sings from treetops to attract a mate

On the move:
migrates at night in flocks of 5–10 birds

What they eat:
insects, seeds and fruit; only visits seed feeders early in spring, when bugs are in short supply

Nest:
cup in a small tree or shrub, low to the ground

Eggs, chicks and childcare:
3–4 pale blue eggs; Mom sits on the eggs and attends to the young

Spends the winter:
migrates to southern Florida, Mexico, Central and South America

REAL QUICK

Size
5½"

Nest
CUP

Feeder
HOPPER

summer
migration
winter

SAW IT!

STAN'S COOL STUFF

The female Indigo Bunting is secretive and plain, so usually only the males are noticed. Females and juveniles return in spring after the males arrive, typically to their nest sites from the previous year. Juveniles move to areas within a mile of their birthplaces.

House Sparrow

Look for the black throat patch

MALE

FEMALE

What to look for:
brown back, gray belly and crown, large black patch from throat to chest; female is light brown with distinct light eyebrows, lacks a throat patch

Where you'll find them:
just about any **habitat**, from cities to farms

Calls and songs:
one of the first birds heard in cities during spring

On the move:
nearly always in small flocks

What they eat:
seeds, insects and fruit; comes to seed feeders

Nest:
cavity; uses dried grass, scraps of plastic, paper and whatever else is available to construct an oversized domed cup within the cavity

Eggs, chicks and childcare:
4–6 white eggs with brown marks; Mom sits on the eggs; Mom and Dad feed the little ones

Spends the winter:
doesn't **migrate**; stays in Florida year-round; moves around to find food

REAL QUICK

Size
6"

Nest
CAVITY

Feeder
TUBE OR HOPPER

year-round

SAW IT!

STAN'S COOL STUFF

The House Sparrow is very comfortable being around people. It was introduced to Central Park in New York City from Europe in 1850. It adjusted to nearly all habitats and now is seen across North America. Populations are decreasing in the U.S. and worldwide.

Eastern Towhee

Look for the rusty sides

FEMALE

MALE

pg. 19

What to look for:
light brown bird with rusty sides, a white belly, white eyes, and a long brown tail with a white tip

Where to find them:
shrubby areas with short trees and thick bushes, backyards and parks

Calls and songs:
calls "tow-hee" distinctly; also has a characteristic **call** that sounds like "drink-your-tea"

On the move:
short flights between shrubby areas and heavy **cover**; flashes white wing patches during flight

What they eat:
insects, seeds and fruit; comes to ground feeders

Nest:
cup; Mom constructs the nest

Eggs, chicks and childcare:
3–4 creamy-white eggs with brown marks; Mom incubates the eggs; Dad and Mom feed the young

Spends the winter:
in Florida, other southern states, Mexico, Central and South America

REAL QUICK

Size
7-8"

Nest
CUP

Feeder
GROUND

year-round

SAW IT!

STAN'S COOL STUFF

The towhee is named for its distinctive "tow-hee" call. It hops backward with both feet, raking leaves to find insects and seeds. In southern coastal states, some have white eyes and others have red eyes. Only the white-eyed variety is found in Florida.

Brown-headed Cowbird

Look for the pointed gray bill

pg. 21

What to look for:
brown bird with a sharp, pointed gray bill

Where you'll find them:
forest edges, open fields, farmlands and backyards

Calls and songs:
sings a low, gurgling song that sounds like water moving; cowbird young are raised by other bird parents, but they still end up singing and calling like their own parents, whom they've never heard

On the move:
Mom flies quietly to another bird's nest, swiftly lays an egg, then flies quickly away

What they eat:
insects and seeds; visits seed feeders

Nest:
doesn't nest; lays eggs in the nests of other birds

Eggs, chicks and childcare:
5–7 white eggs with brown marks; the **host** bird incubates any number of cowbird eggs in her nest and feeds the cowbird young along with her own

Spends the winter:
in Florida and other southern states

REAL QUICK

Size
7½"

Nest
NONE

Feeder
TUBE OR HOPPER

year-round

SAW IT!

STAN'S COOL STUFF

Cowbirds are **brood parasites**, meaning they don't nest or raise their own families. Instead, they lay their eggs in other birds' nests, leaving the host birds to raise their young. Cowbirds have laid their eggs in the nests of more than 200 other bird species.

Cedar Waxwing

Look for the waxy-looking red wing tips

What to look for:
sleek bird with a pointed crest, black mask, light yellow belly and waxy-looking red wing tips; tail has a bold yellow tip; juvenile lacks red wing tips

Where you'll find them:
treetops, forest edges, in trees with fruit

Calls and songs:
constantly makes a high-pitched "sreee" whistling sound while it's perched or in flight

On the move:
flies in flocks of 5–100 birds; moves from area to area, looking for berries

What they eat:
berry-like cedar cones, fruit, seeds and insects

Nest:
cup; Mom and Dad construct it together

Eggs, chicks and childcare:
4–6 pale blue eggs with brown marks; Mom sits on the eggs; Mom and Dad feed the little ones

Spends the winter:
in Florida; wanders around in search of available food supplies

REAL QUICK

Size
7½"

Nest
CUP

Feeder
NONE

winter

SAW IT!

STAN'S COOL STUFF

The waxwing is named for its waxy-looking red wing tips and for the cedar's small, blueberry-like cones that it likes to eat. Before berries are abundant, it eats bugs. The young obtain the mask after their first year of life and red wing tips after their second year.

Sanderling

Look for the short black bill

BREEDING

WINTER
pg. 157

What to look for:

rusty head, chest and back with a white belly, and black legs and bill; white on the wings, seen only in flight

Where you'll find them:

on sandy beaches

Calls and songs:

male gives a high-pitched **call** in flight when he displays to the female

On the move:

when waves retreat at the beach, groups run out to feed; often hops away from people on one leg; performs a distraction **display** when threatened

What they eat:

insects, crabs, worms and small **mollusks**

Nest:

ground nest; Dad builds it

Eggs, chicks and childcare:

3–4 greenish-olive eggs with brown marks; the parents do the **incubation** and feed the kids

Spends the winter:

in coastal Florida, other Gulf Coast states, Mexico and Central America

REAL QUICK

Size
8"

Nest
GROUND

Feeder
NONE

migration
winter

SAW IT!

STAN'S COOL STUFF

The Sanderling is one of the most common shorebirds in Florida. It has breeding **plumage** from April to August and winter plumage from August to April. To rest, it stands on one leg and tucks the other leg into its belly feathers. It nests in the Arctic.

Northern Cardinal

Look for the reddish bill

What to look for:
tan-to-brown bird with a black mask and a large reddish bill; juvenile has a blackish-gray bill

Where you'll find them:
wide variety of habitats, including backyards and parks; usually likes thick **vegetation**

Calls and songs:
calls "whata-cheer-cheer-cheer" in spring; both female and male sing and give chip notes all year

On the move:
short flights from **cover** to cover, often landing on the ground

What they eat:
loves sunflower seeds and enjoys insects, fruit, peanuts and **suet**; visits seed feeders

Nest:
cup of twigs and bark strips, often low in a tree

Eggs, chicks and childcare:
3–4 speckled bluish-white eggs; Mom and Dad share the incubating and feeding duties

Spends the winter:
doesn't **migrate**; gathers with other cardinals and moves around to find good sources of food

REAL QUICK

Size
8–9"

Nest
CUP

Feeder
TUBE OR HOPPER

year-round

SAW IT!

STAN'S COOL STUFF

The Northern Cardinal is one of the few species that has both female and male songsters. Like the males, females sing loud, complex songs. Cardinals are the first to arrive at feeders in the morning and the last to leave before dark.

Red-winged Blackbird

Look for the white eyebrows

What to look for:
heavily streaked with a pointed brown bill and white (sometimes yellow) eyebrows

Where you'll find them:
around marshes, wetlands, lakes and rivers

Calls and songs:
male sings and repeats calls from cattail tops and the surrounding **vegetation**

On the move:
flocks with as many as 10,000 birds gather in autumn, often with other blackbirds

What they eat:
seeds in spring and autumn, insects in summer; visits seed and **suet** feeders

Nest:
cup in a thick stand of cattails over shallow water

Eggs, chicks and childcare:
3–4 speckled bluish-green eggs; Mom does all the incubating, but both parents feed the babies

Spends the winter:
in Florida and other southern states, Mexico and Central America

REAL QUICK

Size
8½"

Nest
CUP

Feeder
TUBE OR HOPPER

year-round

SAW IT!

STAN'S COOL STUFF

During autumn and winter, thousands of these birds gather in farm fields, wetlands and marshes. Come spring, males sing to defend territories and show off their wing patches (**epaulets**) to the females. Later, males can be aggressive when defending their nests.

Burrowing Owl

Look for the big round head

What to look for:
brown owl with bold white spots, a large round head, yellow eyes and very long legs

Where you'll find them:
fields, open backyards, golf courses, airports

Calls and songs:
when threatened, gives a hissing or rattling sound

On the move:
bobs head up and down while doing deep knee bends when upset or threatened; stands or sleeps around the den entrance during the day

What they eat:
bugs and small mammals, reptiles and birds

Nest:
cavity; uses an old underground mammal den and sometimes kicks dirt backward to widen the space; lines the den with cow pies, horse dung, grass and feathers

Eggs, chicks and childcare:
6–11 white eggs; Mom incubates; Mom and Dad feed the **hatchlings**

Spends the winter:
doesn't **migrate**; stays in Florida year-round

REAL QUICK

Size
9–10"

Nest
CAVITY

Feeder
NONE

year-round

SAW IT!

STAN'S COOL STUFF

This owl nests in large family units or in small colonies. You may be able to attract it to your backyard by digging out an artificial den. The male brings food to the incubating female. The family will often move to a new den when the young are a few weeks old.

American Kestrel

Look for the black lines on the face

MALE

FEMALE

What to look for:
rusty back, blue-gray wings, spotted chest, two black lines on the face, a wide black band on the tip of tail; female has rusty wings, dark tail bands

Where you'll find them:
open fields, prairies, farm fields, along highways

Calls and songs:
loud series of high-pitched "klee-klee-klee" calls

On the move:
hovers in midair near roads, then dives for **prey**; pumps tail up and down after landing on a perch

What they eat:
bugs (especially grasshoppers), small animals and birds, reptiles

Nest:
cavity in a tree or wooden nest box; doesn't add nesting material

Eggs, chicks and childcare:
4–5 white eggs with brown marks; parents take turns sitting on the eggs and feeding the babies

Spends the winter:
in Florida and other southern states, Mexico and Central America

REAL QUICK

Size
9–11"

Nest
CAVITY

Feeder
NONE

year-round
winter

SAW IT!

STAN'S COOL STUFF

The kestrel is a small falcon that perches nearly upright. The male and female have different markings—this is unusual for a **raptor**. It can see **ultraviolet light**. That ability helps it find mice and other prey by their urine, which glows bright yellow in ultraviolet light.

Look for the two black neck bands

What to look for:
brown back, white belly, two black bands around the neck like a **necklace**; a bold reddish-orange rump, visible in flight

Where you'll find them:
open country, vacant fields, along railroad tracks, driveways, gravel pits and wetland edges

Calls and songs:
gives a very loud and distinctive "kill-deer" **call**

On the move:
fakes a broken wing to draw intruders away from the nest, and then takes flight once the nest is safe

What they eat:
loves bugs; also eats worms and snails

Nest:
ground; Dad makes just a slight depression in gravel, often very hard to see

Eggs, chicks and childcare:
3–5 tan eggs with brown marks; Dad and Mom incubate the eggs and lead the **hatchlings** to food

Spends the winter:
in Florida and other southern states, Mexico and Central America

REAL QUICK

Size
11"

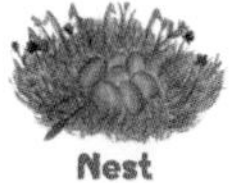

Nest
GROUND

Feeder
NONE

year-round

SAW IT!

STAN'S COOL STUFF

Scientists group the Killdeer in the family of shorebirds, but you're more likely to spot one along railroad tracks, around farms and in other dry habitats than you would at the lakeshore. It's the only shorebird with two black neck bands. It migrates in small flocks.

Brown Thrasher

Look for the long, rusty-red tail

What to look for:
rusty-red bird with a long tail and a long, curved bill, a heavily streaked chest and belly, two white wing bars and bright yellow eyes

Where you'll find them:
thick shrubs, suburban yards and forest edges

Calls and songs:
sings a lot and has many different songs; repeats each phrase in the songs twice

On the move:
quickly flies or runs on the ground in and out of dense shrubs

What they eat:
insects and fruit

Nest:
constructs a cup nest low in a dense shrub or evergreen tree, or in uncultivated **vegetation** along a fence (**fencerow**)

Eggs, chicks and childcare:
4–5 speckled pale blue eggs; Mom and Dad sit on the eggs and feed their young

Spends the winter:
in Florida and other southern states

REAL QUICK

Size
11"

Nest
CUP

Feeder
NONE

year-round

SAW IT!

STAN'S COOL STUFF

The male thrasher is a fantastic songster and sings more songs than any other bird in North America—more than 1,100 tunes in all! It's a noisy feeder due to its habit of turning over leaves, small rocks and branches to find food.

Northern Flicker

Look for the black mustache

What to look for:
brown-and-black bird with a black mustache and black **necklace**, a speckled chest and a red spot on the nape of neck; female lacks a black mustache

Where you'll find them:
forests, small woods, backyards, parks

Calls and songs:
gives a loud "wacka-wacka" **call**

On the move:
flies in a deep, exaggerated up-and-down pattern, flashing yellow under its wings and tail

What they eat:
insects (especially ants and beetles); known to eat the eggs of other birds; visits **suet** feeders

Nest:
cavity in a tree or in a nest box that is stuffed with sawdust; often reuses an old nest several times

Eggs, chicks and childcare:
5–8 white eggs; Mom and Dad incubate the eggs and feed the baby woodpeckers

Spends the winter:
in Florida and other southern states

REAL QUICK

Size
12"

Nest
CAVITY

Feeder
SUET

year-round

SAW IT!

STAN'S COOL STUFF

The Northern Flicker is the only woodpecker to regularly feed on the ground. The male often picks the nest site, usually a natural cavity in a tree. Both parents will pitch in to dig as needed, taking as many as 12 days to finish excavating a hole.

Mourning Dove

Look for the shimmering colors on the neck

What to look for:
brown-to-gray bird with shiny, **iridescent** pink and greenish-blue on the neck, a gray patch on the head, and black spots on the wings and tail

Where you'll find them:
around your seed and ground feeders, open fields

Calls and songs:
known for its soft, sad (mournful) cooing

On the move:
wind rushes through its wing feathers during takeoff and flight, creating a whistling sound

What they eat:
seeds; visits ground and seed feeders

Nest:
flimsy platform in a tree, made with twigs; often falls apart in a storm or during high winds

Eggs, chicks and childcare:
2 white eggs; parents incubate the eggs and feed a regurgitated liquid to their young for the first few days of life

Spends the winter:
in Florida and other southern states

REAL QUICK

Size
12"

Nest
PLATFORM

Feeder
GROUND

year-round

SAW IT!

STAN'S COOL STUFF

The dove is a ground feeder that bobs its head as it walks. It's one of the few birds that drinks without lifting its head, like the Rock Pigeon (pg. 173). Parents **regurgitate** a liquid, called crop-milk, to feed to their young (**squab**) during their first few days of life.

Pied-billed Grebe

Look for the black ring around the bill

Size
12–14"

Nest
GROUND

Feeder
NONE

year-round

What to look for:
small brown waterbird with a black ring on a thick ivory bill and a puffy white patch under the tail; winter **plumage** has a brown bill

Where you'll find them:
ponds and lakes, wetlands

Calls and songs:
a rhythmic series of very loud whooping calls

On the move:
often dives while swimming, entirely submerging itself to catch food; it can reappear on the surface far from where it went under

What they eat:
crayfish, aquatic insects and fish

Nest:
ground nest floating in water

Eggs, chicks and childcare:
5–7 bluish-white eggs; Mom and Dad sit on the eggs and tend to the baby grebes

Spends the winter:
in Florida and other southern states, Mexico and Central America

SAW IT!

STAN'S COOL STUFF

The grebe is well suited to aquatic life. It has short wings, lobed toes, and legs set close to the rear of its body, making it awkward on land. When it's been disturbed, it compresses its feathers to get the air out, and then sinks underwater like a submarine.

Boat-tailed Grackle

Look for the golden-brown head

FEMALE

MALE
pg. 33

What to look for:
golden-brown head and chest, darker wings, a long dark tail and dark eyes, or bright yellow eyes

Where you'll find them:
coastal saltwater marshes and inland marshes

Calls and songs:
noisy, giving several harsh, high-pitched calls and several squeaks

On the move:
travels in large flocks with other blackbirds; flight is typically level, not in an up-and-down pattern

What they eat:
insects, berries, seeds, grains and fish; comes to seed and **suet** feeders

Nest:
cup; Mom makes it with mud or cow dung and grass; nests twice each year in a small **colony**

Eggs, chicks and childcare:
2–4 pale greenish-blue eggs with brown marks; Mom incubates the eggs and feeds the babies

Spends the winter:
doesn't **migrate**; stays in Florida year-round and moves around to find food

REAL QUICK

Size
13–15"

Nest
CUP

Feeder
HOPPER

year-round

SAW IT!

STAN'S COOL STUFF

Boat-tails are sometimes seen picking bugs off the backs of cattle. The birds south of Gainesville have dark eyes; elsewhere in the state they have yellow eyes. They're more common in Florida than the Common Grackle (pg. 27), although their range is smaller.

Willet

Look for the boldly patterned wings

BREEDING

WINTER
pg. 175

What to look for:
brown bird with a white belly, and brown legs and bill; distinctive black-and-white pattern on the wings, seen flashing in flight or during **display**

Where you'll find them:
at the beach

Calls and songs:
calls "pill-will-willet" during the breeding season; gives a "kip-kip-kip" alarm **call** as it takes flight

On the move:
easy to identify due to the black-and-white wing pattern that flashes when the bird flaps rapidly

What they eat:
insects, small fish, small crabs, worms and clams

Nest:
ground nest; Mom builds the nest

Eggs, chicks and childcare:
3–5 olive eggs with dark marks; parents sit on the eggs and feed the young

Spends the winter:
in coastal Florida, other Gulf Coast states and coastal South America

REAL QUICK

Size
14–16"

Nest
GROUND

Feeder
NONE

year-round
winter

SAW IT!

STAN'S COOL STUFF

This bird is seen along the coast and is very common on beaches all winter. It is a medium-sized sandpiper that uses its long bill to probe into sand in search of food. It nests on the ground along the East and Gulf coasts, in some western states and in Canada.

Blue-winged Teal

Look for the white crescent on the face

MALE

FEMALE

What to look for:
brown duck with black speckles, a gray head with a white crescent on the face, a white patch on tail, blue wing patch (**speculum**); female is duller, lacks a white facial crescent and white patch on the tail

REAL QUICK

Size
15-16"

Nest
GROUND

Feeder
NONE

winter

Where you'll find them:
wetlands and lakes

Calls and songs:
male makes a high-pitched squeak; female quacks

On the move:
direct flight to and from water; flocks fly fast in tight formation; female performs a **display** to draw predators away from the nest and young

What they eat:
aquatic plants, seeds and aquatic bugs

Nest:
cozy ground nest some distance from the water

Eggs, chicks and childcare:
8–11 creamy-white eggs; Mom does the **incubation** and feeds the ducklings

Spends the winter:
in Florida and other southern states, Mexico and Central America

SAW IT!

STAN'S COOL STUFF

This is one of the smallest ducks in North America. It migrates farther than most other ducks, nesting as far north as Alaska. The name "Blue-winged" refers to its blue wing patch, which is easiest to see when the bird is in flight.

Red-shouldered Hawk

Look for the reddish shoulders

What to look for:
cinnamon-red head, shoulders, chest and belly, brown wings and back with white spots, and a long tail with black-and-white bands; reddish wing linings, seen in flight

Where you'll find them:
wooded backyards, forest edges, woodlands

Calls and songs:
extremely vocal; gives distinctive, loud screams

On the move:
alternates flapping with gliding

What they eat:
reptiles, amphibians, large insects and small birds

Nest:
large platform made of sticks and lined with sprigs of evergreen or other soft materials; usually in a fork of a large tree

Eggs, chicks and childcare:
2–4 white eggs with dark marks; Mom and Dad sit on the eggs and provide for the youngsters

Spends the winter:
doesn't **migrate** in Florida; stays here year-round

REAL QUICK

Size
15–19"

Nest
PLATFORM

Feeder
NONE

year-round

SAW IT!

STAN'S COOL STUFF

This hawk is common in Florida. It likes to hunt along forest edges and will search for snakes, frogs, bugs and other **prey** as it perches. It stays in the same territory for many years. The parents start to build a nest in February. The young leave the nest (**fledge**) by June.

Ring-necked Duck

Look for the white ring on the bill

FEMALE

MALE
pg. 59

What to look for:
overall brown with a brown back, light brown sides and dark brown crown; face is gray with a white eye-ring, bill has a white ring near the tip, and head is tall with a sloping forehead

Where you'll find them:
usually in larger freshwater lakes rather than saltwater marshes

Calls and songs:
female gives high-pitched peeps; male gives a quick series of grating barks and grunts

On the move:
dives underwater to forage for food; takes to flight by springing up off the water

What they eat:
aquatic plants and insects

Nest:
ground nest; Mom builds it

Eggs, chicks and childcare:
8–10 grayish-to-brown eggs; Mom incubates the eggs and teaches the young how to feed

Spends the winter:
in Florida and other southern states

REAL QUICK

Size
16–18"

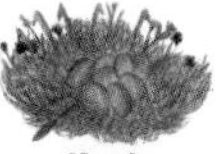

Nest
GROUND

Feeder
NONE

winter

SAW IT!

STAN'S COOL STUFF

The Ring-necked Duck is one of the most abundant winter ducks in Florida. It's also called the Ring-billed Duck due to the obvious ring on its bill. Oddly enough, it was named for the faint rusty collar on its neck, which is nearly impossible to see.

Northern Shoveler

Look for the large, shovel-like bill

FEMALE

MALE
pg. 189

What to look for:
brown duck with black speckles, green wing mark (**speculum**) and a super-large, spoon-shaped bill

Where you'll find them:
shallow wetlands, ponds and small lakes

Calls and songs:
female gives a classic quack; male gives a crazy-sounding combination of popping and quacking, calling "puk-puk, puk-puk, puk-puk"

On the move:
swims in tight circles, stirring up insects to eat; small flocks of 5–10 birds swim with bills pointing toward the water; flocks fly in tight formation

What they eat:
enjoys aquatic insects; likes plants, too

Nest:
ground; Mom forms plant material into a circle

Eggs, chicks and childcare:
9–12 olive eggs; Mom sits on the eggs and leads her little shovelers to food

Spends the winter:
in Florida and other southern states, Mexico and Central America

REAL QUICK

Size
19–21"

Nest
GROUND

Feeder
NONE

winter

SAW IT!

STAN'S COOL STUFF

The Northern Shoveler is a medium-sized duck. It is the only shoveler species found in North America. The name "Shoveler" refers to its peculiar, shovel-like bill. It feeds by using its bill to sift tiny aquatic insects and plants floating on the water's surface.

Mallard

Look for the orange-and-black bill

FEMALE

MOTTLED DUCK

MALE
pg. 191

What to look for:
overall brown duck with an orange-and-black bill, a white tail, and a blue-and-white wing mark (**speculum**), seen best in flight

Where you'll find them:
lakes and ponds, rivers and streams, and maybe even your backyard

Calls and songs:
the sound a duck makes is based on the female Mallard's classic quack; the male doesn't quack

On the move:
sometimes in huge flocks with hundreds of ducks; mostly in small flocks of 6–10, especially in spring

What they eat:
seeds, aquatic plants and insects; visits ground feeders offering corn

Nest:
ground; Mom builds it from plants nearby

Eggs, chicks and childcare:
7–10 greenish-to-whitish eggs; Mom incubates the eggs and leads the young to food

Spends the winter:
in Florida and other southern states

REAL QUICK

Size
19–21"

Nest
GROUND

Feeder
GROUND

year-round

SAW IT!

STAN'S COOL STUFF

This is a dabbling duck, tipping forward in shallow water to feed on aquatic plants on the bottom. Only the female quacks. It will return to its birthplace each year. The Mottled Duck (see inset) looks very much like the female Mallard except for the bill color.

Red-tailed Hawk

Look for the rusty-red tail

What to look for:
plumage varies but it's often brown with a white chest, brown belly band, and a rusty-red tail

Where you'll find them:
just about anywhere; open country, where it flies over open fields and roadsides; cities, where it perches on freeway light posts, fences and trees

Calls and songs:
gives a high-pitched scream that trails off

On the move:
hunts in flight, flying in circles as it searches for **prey**; migrates during the day

What they eat:
mice and other animals, birds, snakes, large bugs

Nest:
large platform made of sticks, lined with materials such as evergreen needles; often in a large tree

Eggs, chicks and childcare:
2–3 white eggs, sometimes speckled; parents sit on the eggs and provide for the youngsters

Spends the winter:
in Florida

REAL QUICK

Size
19–23"

Nest
PLATFORM

Feeder
NONE

year-round

SAW IT!

STAN'S COOL STUFF

This **raptor** is a large hawk with a wide variety of colors from bird to bird, ranging from chocolate to nearly all white. The red color of the tail develops in the second year of life and usually is best seen from above. It returns to the same nest site each year.

Barred Owl

Look for the dark eyes

What to look for:
brown-to-gray owl with dark brown eyes, dark horizontal bars on upper chest, vertical streaks on the lower chest and belly, yellow bill and feet

Where you'll find them:
dense woodlands

Calls and songs:
gives calls of 6–8 hoots, sounding something like "who-who-who-cooks-for-you"

On the move:
a smooth and silent flight, gliding on flat, outstretched wings; often hunts during the day, perching and watching for mice and other **prey**

What they eat:
small mammals, birds, fish, reptiles, amphibians

Nest:
natural cavity in a tree or uses a nest box with a large entrance hole; doesn't add nesting material

Eggs, chicks and childcare:
2–3 white eggs; Mom sits on the eggs; Mom and Dad attend to the babies

Spends the winter:
doesn't **migrate**; stays in Florida year-round

REAL QUICK

Size
20-24"

Nest
CAVITY

Feeder
NONE

year-round

SAW IT!

STAN'S COOL STUFF

The Barred Owl is the only dark-eyed owl in Florida, but it's very common. It's a chunky bird with a large head. It fishes by hovering over water, and then reaches down to grab one. After the young **fledge**, they stay with their parents for up to four months.

Great Horned Owl

Look for the feather tufts on the head

What to look for:
"eared" owl with large yellow eyes, a V-shaped white throat and horizontal barring on the chest

Where you'll find them:
just about any **habitat** throughout Florida

Calls and songs:
calls a familiar "hoo-hoo-hoo-hoooo"

On the move:
flies silently on big wings that stretch out to 4 feet; takes a few quick flaps, and then glides

What they eat:
small to medium mammals, birds (especially ducks), snakes and insects

Nest:
no nest; takes over the nest of another bird or uses a broken tree stump or other semi-cavity

Eggs, chicks and childcare:
2–3 white eggs, laid in January and February; Mom incubates; Dad and Mom feed the **hatchlings**

Spends the winter:
doesn't **migrate** and usually hangs around the same area year after year

REAL QUICK

Size
21-25"

Nest
NONE

Feeder
NONE

year-round

SAW IT!

STAN'S COOL STUFF

The "**horns**" of the Great Horned are feather tufts, not ears. Its eyelids close from the top down, like ours. It has fabulous hearing and can hear a mouse moving under a deep pile of leaves. It's one of the few animals that will kill a skunk or a porcupine.

Wild Turkey

Look for the bare blue-and-red head

MALE

FEMALE

What to look for:
funny-looking brown-and-bronze bird, bare blue-and-red head, long thin beard, large fanning tail; female is thinner, duller and often lacks a beard

Where you'll find them:
just about any **habitat**, from suburban yards to prairies and forests

Calls and songs:
a fast, descending "gobble-gobble-gobble-gobble" that's often heard before the bird is seen

On the move:
a strong flier that can approach 60 mph; also able to fly straight up, and then away

What they eat:
insects, seeds and fruit

Nest:
ground; Mom scrapes out a shallow depression and pads it with soft leaves

Eggs, chicks and childcare:
10–12 whitish eggs with dull brown marks; Mom sits on the eggs and leads the babies to food

Spends the winter:
moves around Florida to find **cover** and food

REAL QUICK

Size
36–48"

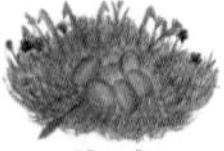

Nest
GROUND

Feeder
NONE

year-round

SAW IT!

STAN'S COOL STUFF

This is the largest game bird in Florida. The average turkey has 5,000–6,000 feathers. It sees three times better than people, and it can hear sounds from a mile away. A male will lead a group of up to 20 females. Male turkeys are called toms. Females are hens.

Brown Pelican

Look for the huge gray bill

BREEDING

NON-BREEDING

What to look for:
gray-brown body with a black belly, a very long gray bill, a white or yellow head, and dark rust on the back of the neck during breeding season; non-breeding back of the neck is white

Where you'll find them:
at the beach

Calls and songs:
silent; snaps the upper bill and lower bill together to make a loud popping sound

On the move:
often sits on posts at beachside docks

What they eat:
fish; occasionally amphibians and eggs

Nest:
ground nest, in a large **colony**, often on an island

Eggs, chicks and childcare:
2–4 white eggs; Mom and Dad incubate the eggs and share the childcare

Spends the winter:
along coastal Florida

REAL QUICK

Size
46-50"

Nest
GROUND

Feeder
NONE

year-round

SAW IT!

STAN'S COOL STUFF

This bird is common in Florida, although it was endangered not long ago due to the use of pesticides. It hunts by diving headfirst into the ocean. Then it opens its bill and sweeps fish into its mouth with the expandable pouch on the bottom of its bill, like a net.

Brown-headed Nuthatch

What to look for:
tiny bird with a brown head, dull white chin, chest and belly, and a gray back

Where you'll find them:
open pine forests, woodlands, parks, backyards, forest edges

Calls and songs:
a characteristic spring **call**, "whi-whi-whi-whi," given during February and March

On the move:
creeps down tree trunks and branches headfirst, searching for hidden insects and insect eggs; makes quick, short flights from tree to tree

What they eat:
insects and seeds; visits seed and **suet** feeders

Nest:
cavity; parents **excavate** or will use a vacant woodpecker hole, a natural cavity or a nest box

Eggs, chicks and childcare:
3–5 white eggs with dark marks; Mom sits on the eggs; Mom and Dad feed the young

Spends the winter:
doesn't **migrate**; moves around to find food

REAL QUICK

Size
$4\frac{1}{2}$"

Nest
CAVITY

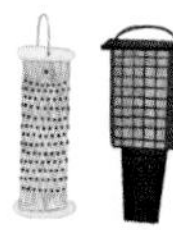

Feeder
TUBE OR SUET

year-round

SAW IT!

STAN'S COOL STUFF

The Brown-headed Nuthatch has an extra-long hind toe claw, called a nail, on each foot, giving it the ability to cling to trees and climb down headfirst. It works hard to remove seeds from pinecones. Pairs defend a very small territory all year.

Carolina Chickadee

Look for the black cap

What to look for:
mostly gray bird with a black cap and throat patch, tan sides and belly, and a whitish chest

Where you'll find them:
nearly all habitats—just look around for this bird

Calls and songs:
calls "chika-dee-dee-dee-dee"; also gives a high-pitched, two-toned "fee-bee" **call** during spring; can have different calls in different regions

On the move:
flies short distances with short, fluttery wings

What they eat:
seeds, bugs and fruit; visits seed and **suet** feeders

Nest:
excavates a cavity or uses a nest box; gathers mostly green moss for the nest and fur to line it

Eggs, chicks and childcare:
5–7 white eggs with reddish-brown marks; Mom and Dad sit on the eggs and feed their **brood**

Spends the winter:
doesn't **migrate**; moves around to forage for food and shelter instead; must feed every day in winter and forges for food even during the worst storms

REAL QUICK

Size
5"

Nest
CAVITY

Feeder
TUBE OR SUET

year-round

SAW IT!

STAN'S COOL STUFF

You can attract this bird with a seed feeder or nest box. Usually it's the first to find a new feeder. It's easily tamed and hand fed. Much of its diet comes from bird feeders, so it can be a common urban bird. It's often seen with nuthatches, woodpeckers and other birds.

Yellow-rumped Warbler

Look for the bright yellow patches

MALE

What to look for:
gray with black streaks on the chest and yellow patches on head, flanks and rump; female is duller gray; first winter juvenile is similar to the female

Where you'll find them:
can be seen in any **habitat** during migration; seems to prefer **deciduous** forests and forest edges

Calls and songs:
sings a wonderful song in spring; calls a single robust "chip," heard mostly during migration

On the move:
quickly moves among trees and from the ground to trees; flits around upper branches of tall trees

What they eat:
insects and berries; visits **suet** feeders in spring

Nest:
cup; Mom builds the nest on her own in forests

Eggs, chicks and childcare:
4–5 white eggs with brown marks; Mom sits on the eggs; Mom and Dad feed the young

Spends the winter:
in Florida and other southern states, Mexico and Central America

REAL QUICK

Size
5–6"

Nest
CUP

Feeder
SUET

winter

SAW IT!

STAN'S COOL STUFF

This bird is also called the Myrtle Warbler. It is one of the last warblers to arrive in winter and one of the first to leave in spring. The male molts his gray feathers in fall, changing to a dull color like the female for the winter. He keeps his yellow patches all year.

Tufted Titmouse

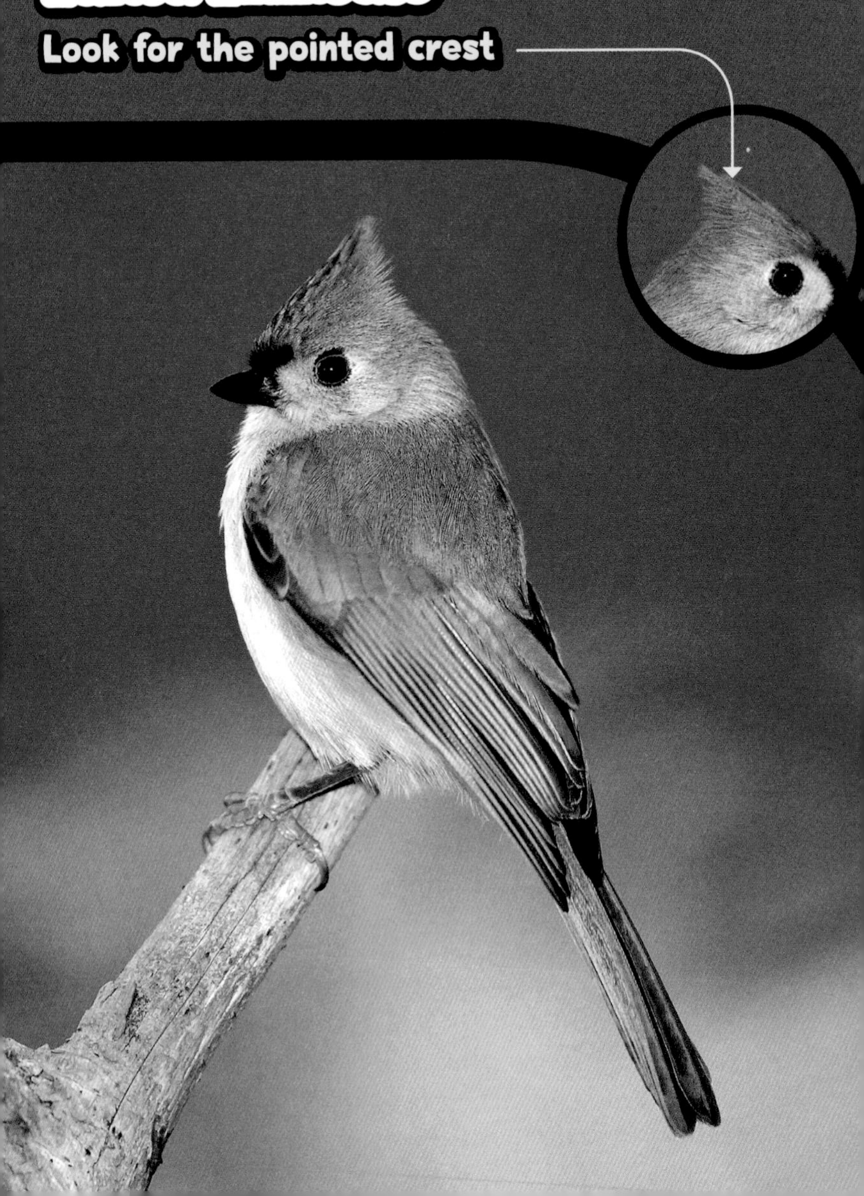
Look for the pointed crest

What to look for:
gray bird with a white chest and belly, a rusty-brown wash on the flanks and a pointed crest

Where to find them:
woodlands, backyards and parks

Calls and songs:
quickly repeats a loud "peter-peter-peter" **call**

On the move:
usually seen only one or two at a time, never in big flocks, moving through thick forests and along forest edges

What they eat:
insects, seeds (especially black oil sunflower seeds) and fruit; visits seed and **suet** feeders

Nest:
cavity; boldly pulls hair from sleeping dogs, cats or squirrels and uses it to line an old woodpecker hole or a nest box

Eggs, chicks and childcare:
5–7 white eggs with brown marks; Mom sits on the eggs, and Mom and Dad feed the young

Spends the winter:
doesn't **migrate**; stays in Florida year-round

REAL QUICK

Size
6"

Nest
CAVITY

Feeder
TUBE OR SUET

year-round

SAW IT!

STAN'S COOL STUFF

The titmouse is a common feeder bird. You can attract it by filling a feeder with black oil sunflower seeds or by putting up a nest box. It's usually seen only one or two at a time. The male feeds the female during courtship and nesting. Its name means "small bird."

Common Ground-Dove

What to look for:
small gray-to-tan dove with a short tail, and a reddish-orange bill with a black tip; bold chestnut wing linings, seen in flight

Where you'll find them:
open dry woodlands, old fields and pastures

Calls and songs:
a series of soft coos; often coos while displaying

On the move:
often seen in pairs; walks around like a wind-up toy, bobbing its head and shuffling its feet; spends most of its time on the ground

What they eat:
seeds and berries; visits ground and seed feeders

Nest:
ground nest; sometimes builds a flimsy nest in a shrub or takes an empty nest that's low in a tree

Eggs, chicks and childcare:
2–4 white eggs; Mom and Dad sit on the eggs and **regurgitate** a liquid, called crop-milk, to feed to the young (**squab**) for their first few days of life

Spends the winter:
doesn't **migrate**; stays in Florida year-round

REAL QUICK

Size
6½"

Nest
GROUND

Feeder
GROUND

year-round

SAW IT!

STAN'S COOL STUFF

This is the smallest dove species in Florida. You can see it foraging around your bird feeders, scratching for seeds. It's not afraid of people, so you can get a good look at it while it looks for food. In the past it was known as the Eastern Ground-Dove.

Sanderling

Look for the gray back

WINTER

BREEDING
pg. 103

What to look for:
a light-colored sandpiper with a gray head and back, white belly, and black legs and bill; white stripe on the wings, seen only in flight

Where you'll find them:
on sandy beaches

Calls and songs:
gives a fast, high-pitched squeak just before taking flight and just after takeoff

On the move:
when waves retreat at the beach, groups run out to feed; often hops away from people on one leg; performs a distraction **display** when threatened

What they eat:
insects, crabs, worms and small **mollusks**

Nest:
ground nest; Dad builds it

Eggs, chicks and childcare:
3–4 greenish-olive eggs with brown marks; the parents do the **incubation** and feed the kids

Spends the winter:
in coastal Florida, other Gulf Coast states, Mexico and Central America

REAL QUICK

Size
8"

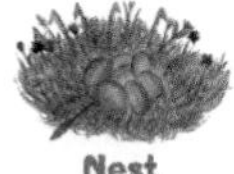

Nest
GROUND

Feeder
NONE

migration
winter

SAW IT!

STAN'S COOL STUFF

The Sanderling is one of the most common shorebirds in Florida. It has winter **plumage** from August to April and breeding plumage from April to August. To rest, it stands on one leg and tucks the other leg into its belly feathers. It nests in the Arctic.

Eastern Screech-Owl

Look for the feathered "ear" tufts

GRAY MORPH

RED MORPH

What to look for:
small "eared" owl with two different speckled colorations: gray-and-white and red-and-white

Where you'll find them:
any type of forest, as long as it has some natural cavities suitable for roosting and nesting

Calls and songs:
a trembling, descending **trill**, like a sound effect in a scary movie; seldom gives a screeching **call**

On the move:
flies silently on short, rapidly flapping wings; active from dusk to dawn

What they eat:
large bugs, small mammals, birds and snakes

Nest:
cavity; uses an old woodpecker hole or a wooden nest box and doesn't add nesting material

Eggs, chicks and childcare:
4–5 white eggs; Mom sits on the eggs to incubate; Dad feeds Mom and the newly hatched babies

Spends the winter:
doesn't **migrate**; stays in Florida year-round but has a different territory in winter than in summer

REAL QUICK

Size
8–10"

Nest
CAVITY

Feeder
NONE

year-round

SAW IT!

STAN'S COOL STUFF

This little owl has excellent hearing and eyesight. On winter days, it will sun itself at a nest box entrance hole. The male and female may roost with each other at night and may have a long-term **pair bond**. The gray **morph** is more common than the red variety.

Gray Catbird

Look for the black crown

What to look for:
gray bird with a black crown and long, thin black bill; often lifts its tail, exposing a chestnut patch

Where you'll find them:
thick shrubs, forest edges, backyards, parks

Calls and songs:
gives a rasping **call** that sounds like a house cat meowing; often mimics other birds

On the move:
quickly zips back into shrubs if approached

What they eat:
insects and occasional fruit; visits suet feeders

Nest:
cup of small twigs in thick shrubs; often adds a scrap of plastic to the twigs

Eggs, chicks and childcare:
4–6 blue-green eggs; Mom incubates the eggs; Mom and Dad take turns feeding the chicks, but because the parents look the same, it's hard to tell who's doing the feeding!

Spends the winter:
in Florida and other southern states; many are year-round residents in Florida

REAL QUICK

Size
9"

Nest
CUP

Feeder
SUET

year-round
winter

SAW IT!

STAN'S COOL STUFF

This handsome, secretive bird is more often heard than seen. The Chippewa Indian name for it means "the bird that cries with grief." Once you've heard the call, you won't forget it. If a cowbird lays an egg in a catbird nest, the catbird will break it and eject it.

Loggerhead Shrike

What to look for:

gray head and back with a white chin, chest and belly; black wings, tail, legs and feet, with a black mask across the eyes and a hooked black bill

Where you'll find them:

coniferous trees, barbed wire fences and bird feeders, where it hunts small birds

Calls and songs:

doesn't sing; repeats harsh phrases lacking melody

On the move:

to hunt, it swoops down on **prey**, grasps it with the feet, hammers at it with its bill and carries it to a storage spot, where it's kept for eating later

What they eat:

insects (especially grasshoppers), lizards, small mammals and birds, frogs

Nest:

cup; Dad and Mom build it together

Eggs, chicks and childcare:

4–7 off-white eggs with dark marks; Mom sits on the eggs; Mom and Dad feed the baby birds

Spends the winter:

migrants join the many year-round residents

REAL QUICK

Size
9"

Nest
CUP

Feeder
NONE

year-round

SAW IT!

STAN'S COOL STUFF

The shrike is a songbird that's also called the Butcher Bird. It acts more like a **raptor** than a songster. It has weak feet, so it skewers its prey on thorns or other sharp objects. This fastens the item for eating later and keeps it still when it tears off pieces to eat.

American Robin

Look for the rusty-red breast

MALE

FEMALE

What to look for:
black head and a rich, rusty-red breast; female is duller with a gray head and lighter breast

Where you'll find them:
loves to hop on lawns in search of worms

Calls and songs:
chips and chirps; sings all night in spring; studies report that city robins sing louder than country robins so they can be heard over traffic and noise

On the move:
found all over the U.S. in an amazing range of habitats, from sea level to mountaintops

What they eat:
insects, fruit and berries, as well as earthworms

Nest:
cup; weaves plant materials and uses mud to plaster the nest to a sheltered location

Eggs, chicks and childcare:
4–7 pale blue eggs; Mom sits on the eggs; Mom and Dad feed the baby robins

Spends the winter:
in Florida and other southern states, Mexico and Central America

REAL QUICK

Size
9–11"

Nest
CUP

Feeder
NONE

year-round
winter

SAW IT!

STAN'S COOL STUFF

When a robin walks across your lawn and turns its head to the side, it isn't listening for worms—it is looking for them. Because its eyes are on the sides of its head, a robin must focus its sight out of one eye to see the dirt moving caused by a moving worm.

Northern Mockingbird
Look for the white wing patches

What to look for:
silver-gray head and back, a light gray chest and belly, white wing patches, a mostly black tail with white outer tail feathers

Where to find them:
on top of a shrub, where it sits for long periods; parks and yards

Calls and songs:
imitates or mocks other birds (vocal mimicry); young males often sing at night

On the move:
very lively, spreading its wings, flashing its white wing patches and wagging its tail; wing patches flash during flight or **display**

What they eat:
insects and fruit

Nest:
cup; Mom and Dad work together to build it

Eggs, chicks and childcare:
3–5 speckled blue-green eggs; Mom sits on the eggs to incubate; Mom and Dad feed their young

Spends the winter:
in Florida and other southern states

REAL QUICK

Size
10"

Nest
CUP

Feeder
NONE

year-round

SAW IT!

STAN'S COOL STUFF

Mockingbirds perform a fantastic mating dance. Pairs hold up their heads and tails and run toward each other. They flash their wing patches, and then retreat to nearby **cover**. Usually they're not afraid of people, so you may be able to get a close look.

Black-bellied Plover

Look for the white belly

WINTER

BREEDING
pg. 57

What to look for:
light gray bird with a white chest and belly, a faint white eyebrow mark, and black legs and bill

Where you'll find them:
at the beach

Calls and songs:
calls a single high-pitched, slurred "fee-a-wee"

On the move:
often darts across the ground to grab a bug and run off with it; male performs a butterfly-like courtship flight to attract females

What they eat:
insects, worms, clams and **crustaceans**

Nest:
ground nest; Dad and Mom construct it together

Eggs, chicks and childcare:
3–4 pinkish or greenish eggs with blackish-brown marks; parents incubate the eggs; Dad feeds the kids, who quickly learn how to feed themselves

Spends the winter:
along coastal Florida

REAL QUICK

Size
11–12"

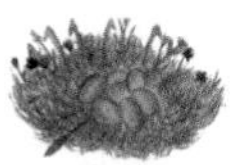

Nest
GROUND

Feeder
NONE

migration
winter

SAW IT!

STAN'S COOL STUFF

The fall migrators start arriving in Florida in July and August. During flight, this bird displays a white rump and a white stripe on its wings. It starts breeding at 3 years of age. The female leaves her mate and their young about 12 days after the eggs hatch.

Eurasian Collared-Dove

Look for the black collar on the back of neck

What to look for:
pale gray bird with a slightly darker back, wings and tail, and a black collar on the nape of neck; tail is long and squared off at the end

Where you'll find them:
wherever it can scratch for seeds

Calls and songs:
gives a series of coos, often during a **display**

On the move:
usually found in small to large flocks; fast flaps, then glides with wings in a V

What they eat:
seeds and fruit; visits ground and seed feeders

Nest:
platform on a building, balcony, barn or shed, or under a bridge; Mom and Dad construct it

Eggs, chicks and childcare:
3–5 white creamy-white eggs; Mom and Dad sit on the eggs and **regurgitate** a liquid food, called crop-milk, to feed to the young (**squab**) during their first few days of life

Spends the winter:
doesn't **migrate**; stays in Florida year-round

REAL QUICK

Size
12½"

Nest
PLATFORM

Feeder
GROUND

year-round

SAW IT!

STAN'S COOL STUFF

This dove is originally from Asia. It increased its range to include Europe, and then people brought it into the Bahamas. From there it flew to Florida. Scientists believe that this bird will continue to expand its range across North America like it did across Europe.

Rock Pigeon

Look for the gleaming, iridescent patches

What to look for:
color pattern varies; usually shades of gray with gleaming, **iridescent** patches of green mixed with blue; often has a light rump patch

Where you'll find them:
nearly anyplace where it can scratch for seeds

Calls and songs:
a series of coos, usually given during a **display**

On the move:
typically in small to large flocks; flaps rapidly, then glides with wings in a V shape

What they eat:
seeds and fruit; visits ground and seed feeders

Nest:
platform on a building, balcony, barn or shed, or under a bridge

Eggs, chicks and childcare:
1–2 white eggs; Mom and Dad sit on the eggs and **regurgitate** a liquid, called crop-milk, to feed to the young (**squab**) for their first few days of life

Spends the winter:
doesn't **migrate**; stays in Florida year-round

REAL QUICK

Size
13"

Nest
PLATFORM

Feeder
GROUND

year-round

SAW IT!

STAN'S COOL STUFF

The pigeon was introduced to North America by the early settlers from Europe. Years of breeding in captivity have made it one of the few birds that has a variety of colors. It's also one of the few birds that can drink without tilting its head back.

Look for the boldly patterned wings

WINTER

BREEDING
pg. 125

What to look for:
gray bird with a white belly, and gray legs and bill; distinctive black-and-white pattern on the wings, seen flashing in flight or during **display**

Where you'll find them:
at the beach

Calls and songs:
calls "pill-will-willet" during the breeding season; gives a "kip-kip-kip" alarm **call** as it takes flight

On the move:
easy to identify due to the black-and-white wing pattern that flashes when the bird flaps rapidly

What they eat:
insects, small fish, small crabs, worms and clams

Nest:
ground nest; Mom builds the nest

Eggs, chicks and childcare:
3–5 olive eggs with dark marks; parents sit on the eggs and feed the young

Spends the winter:
in coastal Florida, other Gulf Coast states and coastal South America

REAL QUICK

Size
14–16"

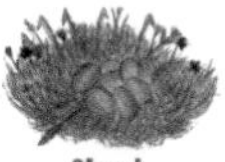

Nest
GROUND

Feeder
NONE

year-round
winter

SAW IT!

STAN'S COOL STUFF

This bird is seen along the coast and is very common on beaches all winter. It is a medium-sized sandpiper that uses its long bill to probe into sand in search of food. It nests on the ground along the East and Gulf coasts, in some western states and in Canada.

Great Blue Heron
Look for the long yellow bill

What to look for:
tall gray heron with black eyebrows that end in plumes off the back of the head, neck feathers that drop down like a **necklace**, and a long yellow bill

Where you'll find them:
open water, from small ponds to large lakes

Calls and songs:
when startled, it barks repeatedly like a dog and keeps at it while flying away

On the move:
holds its neck in an S shape in flight and slightly cups its wings, trailing its legs straight out behind

What they eat:
small fish, frogs, insects, snakes and baby birds

Nest:
platform in a tree near or over open water, in a **colony** of up to 100 birds

Eggs, chicks and childcare:
3–5 blue-green eggs; parents incubate the eggs and feed the **brood**

Spends the winter:
in Florida, other southern states, Mexico, Central and South America

REAL QUICK

Size
42–48"

Nest
PLATFORM

Feeder
NONE

year-round

SAW IT!

STAN'S COOL STUFF

This is the tallest heron in Florida and very common. It stalks fish in shallow water and strikes at mice, squirrels and anything else it can capture on land. Red-winged Blackbirds (pg. 25) often attack it to prevent it from taking their babies out of their nests.

Sandhill Crane

Look for the red cap

What to look for:
super-tall gray crane with long legs and neck, and a scarlet-red cap; wings and body are often stained rusty-brown

Where you'll find them:
wetlands, small and large

Calls and songs:
a very loud and distinctive rattling **call**, often heard before the bird is seen; call is one of the loudest due to a very long windpipe (**trachea**)

On the move:
wings look like they're flicking in flight, with the upstroke quicker than the downstroke; can fly at great heights of over 10,000 feet

What they eat:
insects, fruit, worms, plants and amphibians

Nest:
ground nest of aquatic plants shaped into a mound

Eggs, chicks and childcare:
2 olive eggs with brown marks; Mom and Dad sit on the eggs; to get fed, babies follow their parents

Spends the winter:
in Florida, other southern states and Mexico

REAL QUICK

Size
42–48"

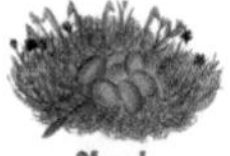

Nest
GROUND

Feeder
NONE

year-round
migration
winter

SAW IT!

STAN'S COOL STUFF

The Sandhill is one of the tallest birds in the country. It works mud into its feathers, staining them a rusty color. Sandhills do a cool mating dance: a pair will first bow, then jump, cackle loudly, flap their wings, and finally, flip sticks and grass into the air.

Ruby-throated Hummingbird

Look for the gleaming ruby-red throat

MALE

FEMALE

What to look for:
tiny **iridescent** green bird with a black throat patch that shimmers bright ruby-red in direct sunlight; female lacks the throat patch

Where you'll find them:
many habitats, from yards and parks to forests

Calls and songs:
will chatter or buzz to communicate; doesn't sing or hum a melody—it's the incredibly fast flapping wings that create the humming sound

On the move:
the only bird that can fly backward; also hovers in midair and flies straight up and straight down!

What they eat:
nectar and insects; visits nectar feeders

Nest:
stretchy cup of plant materials and spiderwebs; glues bits of **lichen** to the outside for camouflage

Eggs, chicks and childcare:
2 white eggs; Mom does all egg and chick care

Spends the winter:
in southern Florida, other southern states, Mexico and Central America

REAL QUICK

Size
3–3½"

Nest
CUP

Feeder
NECTAR

summer
winter

SAW IT!

STAN'S COOL STUFF

This is the tiniest bird in the state, with approximately the same weight as a U.S. penny. It flaps 50–60 times per second or more in normal flight. It breathes 250 times per minute, and its heart beats 1,260 times per minute! It feeds at colorful tube-shaped flowers.

Look for the vivid blue head

MALE

FEMALE

What to look for:
vivid blue head, a lime-green back and an orange-to-red chest and belly, with dark wings and tail; female is bright green above, light green below

Where you'll find them:
backyard gardens, brushy roads, thick hedges, woodlands with lots of **vegetation**, scrublands

Calls and songs:
sings loud warbling phrases

On the move:
male flies with exaggerated wing beats, quivers his wings and bows his head to **display** to female

What they eat:
seeds, insects; visits seed feeders in wooded yards

Nest:
cup made of grass and lined with animal hair; usually in a deep, tangled mass of vines

Eggs, chicks and childcare:
3–5 pale blue eggs with brown marks; Mom sits on the eggs; Mom and Dad feed the babies

Spends the winter:
in Florida, other southern states, Cuba, Jamaica, the Bahamas, Mexico, Central and South America

REAL QUICK

Size
5½"

Nest
CUP

Feeder
HOPPER

summer
migration
winter

SAW IT!

STAN'S COOL STUFF

No other bird can compare with the striking colors of the male Painted Bunting. The female is also hard to confuse with other birds. Shy, the male and female move around on the ground under a tangle of branches or through leafy growth without being seen.

Monk Parakeet

Look for the lime-green back

What to look for:

lime-green back with a lighter green belly, gray forehead, throat and chest, blue on wings, a short, hooked yellow bill and long, narrow tail

Where you'll find them:

urban and suburban areas, especially parks

Calls and songs:

gives many different calls; groups give a series of loud squawks, making lots of noise

On the move:

each foot has two toes pointing forward and two toes pointing back; this arrangement helps the bird hold food and bring it up to its mouth

What they eat:

seeds; visits seed feeders

Nest:

cavity, in a **colony**; the colony shares one very big stick nest, where the birds nest in their own cavity

Eggs, chicks and childcare:

4–6 off-white eggs; Mom incubates the eggs by herself, but Dad helps her feed the young

Spends the winter:

doesn't **migrate**; stays in Florida year-round

REAL QUICK

Size
12"

Nest
CAVITY

Feeder
HOPPER

year-round

SAW IT!

STAN'S COOL STUFF

There are more than 300 species of parakeets in the world. Monk Parakeets were originally brought to Florida from Argentina as pets. Over time, the birds escaped or were allowed to fly away. Today, these parakeets live with each other in colonies.

Green Heron

Look for the rusty-red chest

What to look for:
short, stocky heron with a blue-green back, a dark green crest, and a rusty-red chest and neck; short orange legs turn yellow after the breeding season

Where you'll find them:
ponds, wetlands, small lakes and rivers

Calls and songs:
often gives an explosive, rasping "skyew" **call** when startled

On the move:
waits on the shore or wades stealthily, hunting for food; makes short, quick flights across the water

What they eat:
small fish, aquatic insects, amphibians

Nest:
platform of sticks in a **coniferous** or **deciduous** tree, often a short distance from water and can be very high in the tree

Eggs, chicks and childcare:
2–4 light green eggs; parents share the childcare

Spends the winter:
in Florida, other southern states, Mexico, Central and South America

REAL QUICK

Size
16–22"

Nest
PLATFORM

Feeder
NONE

year-round
summer

SAW IT!

STAN'S COOL STUFF

The Green Heron holds its head very close to its body. When it's excited, it raises its crest. To catch fish, it will place an object, such as an insect, on the surface of the water as bait. Baby herons make a loud ticking sound, like the ticktock of a clock.

Northern Shoveler

Look for the large, shovel-like bill

MALE

FEMALE
pg. 133

What to look for:
shiny, **iridescent** green head with rusty sides, a white chest and a super-large, spoon-shaped bill

Where you'll find them:
shallow wetlands, ponds and small lakes

Calls and songs:
male gives a crazy-sounding combination of popping and quacking, calling "puk-puk, puk-puk, puk-puk"; female gives a classic quack **call**

On the move:
swims in tight circles, stirring up insects to eat; small flocks of 5–10 birds swim with bills pointing toward the water; flocks fly in tight formation

What they eat:
enjoys aquatic insects; likes plants, too

Nest:
ground; Mom forms plant material into a circle

Eggs, chicks and childcare:
9–12 olive eggs; Mom sits on the eggs and leads her little shovelers to food

Spends the winter:
in Florida and other southern states, Mexico and Central America

REAL QUICK

Size
19–21"

Nest
GROUND

Feeder
NONE

winter

SAW IT!

STAN'S COOL STUFF

The Northern Shoveler is a medium-sized duck. It is the only shoveler species found in North America. The name "Shoveler" refers to its peculiar, shovel-like bill. It feeds by using its bill to sift tiny aquatic insects and plants floating on the water's surface.

Look for the green head

MALE

FEMALE
pg. 135

What to look for:

green head with a white **necklace**, rusty-brown chest, gray sides, yellow bill, orange legs and feet

Where you'll find them:

lakes and ponds, rivers and streams, and maybe even your backyard

Calls and songs:

the male doesn't quack; when you think of how a duck sounds, it's based on the female Mallard's classic loud quack

On the move:

sometimes in huge flocks with hundreds of ducks; mostly in small flocks of 6–10, especially in spring

What they eat:

seeds, aquatic plants and insects; visits ground feeders offering corn

Nest:

ground; Mom builds it from plants nearby

Eggs, chicks and childcare:

7–10 greenish-to-whitish eggs; Mom incubates the eggs and leads the young to food

Spends the winter:

in Florida and other southern states

REAL QUICK

Size
19–21"

Nest
GROUND

Feeder
GROUND

year-round

SAW IT!

STAN'S COOL STUFF

This is a dabbling duck, tipping forward in shallow water to eat plants on the bottom. Only the male has black feathers in the center of its tail that curl upward. The name "Mallard" means "male" and refers to the males, which don't help raise their young.

Baltimore Oriole

Look for the black head

What to look for:
flaming orange bird with a black head and back, and black wings with white wing bars

Where you'll find them:
parks, yards and forests; in treetops, where it feeds on caterpillars

Calls and songs:
a fantastic songster, singing loudly; often heard before it is seen

On the move:
often returns to the same area year after year

What they eat:
insects, fruit and **nectar**; comes to nectar, orange half and grape jelly feeders

Nest:
pendulous; an interesting nest that looks like a sock hanging from an outer branch of a tall tree

Eggs, chicks and childcare:
4–5 bluish eggs with brown marks; Mom sits on the eggs; Mom and Dad do the childcare

Spends the winter:
flies to the southern half of Florida; also goes to Mexico, Central America and South America

REAL QUICK

Size
7–8"

Nest
PENDULOUS

Feeder
NECTAR

migration
winter

SAW IT!

STAN'S COOL STUFF

Orioles visit feeders that offer sugar water (nectar), orange halves or grape jelly. Parents bring their young to feeders. Young males turn orange and black at 1½ years. Orioles are some of the first birds to arrive in winter and some of the last to leave in spring.

House Finch

Look for the reddish face and the brown cap

pg. 87

What to look for:
red-to-orange face, throat, chest and rump, and a brown cap

Where you'll find them:
forests, city and suburban areas, around homes, parks and farms

Calls and songs:
male sings a loud, cheerful warbling song

On the move:
moves around in small family units; never travels long distances

What they eat:
seeds, fruit and leaf buds; comes to seed feeders and feeders with a glop of grape jelly

Nest:
cup, but occasionally in a cavity; likes to nest in a hanging flower basket or on a front door wreath

Eggs, chicks and childcare:
4–5 pale blue eggs, lightly marked; Mom sits on the eggs and Dad feeds her while she incubates; Mom and Dad feed the **brood**

Spends the winter:
in most of Florida; moves around to find food

REAL QUICK

Size
5"

Nest
CUP

Feeder
TUBE OR HOPPER

year-round

SAW IT!

STAN'S COOL STUFF

The House Finch is very social and is found across the country. It can be a common bird at feeders. Unfortunately, it suffers from a fatal eye disease that causes the eyes to crust over. It's rare to see a yellow male; yellow **plumage** may be a result of a poor diet.

Northern Cardinal

Look for the black mask

MALE

pg. 105

What to look for:
all-red bird with a black mask, and a large red crest and bill

Where you'll find them:
wide variety of habitats including backyards and parks; usually likes thick **vegetation**

Calls and songs:
calls "whata-cheer-cheer-cheer" in spring; both male and female sing and give chip notes all year

On the move:
short flights from **cover** to cover, often landing on the ground

What they eat:
loves sunflower seeds and enjoys insects, fruit, peanuts and **suet**; visits seed feeders

Nest:
cup of twigs and bark strips, often low in a tree

Eggs, chicks and childcare:
3–4 speckled bluish-white eggs; Mom and Dad share the incubating and feeding duties

Spends the winter:
doesn't **migrate**; gathers with other cardinals and moves around to find good sources of food

REAL QUICK

Size
8-9"

Nest
CUP

Feeder
TUBE OR HOPPER

year-round

SAW IT!

STAN'S COOL STUFF

The Northern Cardinal is one of the few species that has both male and female songsters. Like the females, males sing loud, complex songs. Cardinals are the first to arrive at feeders in the morning and the last to leave before dark.

Roseate Spoonbill

Look for the flat, spoon-shaped bill

REAL QUICK

Size
30–34"

Nest
PLATFORM

Feeder
NONE

year-round
winter

What to look for:

overall pink with red highlights, a white neck with a black patch on the back of the head, a heavy, spoon-shaped flat bill and long red legs; juvenile is paler than the adult

Where you'll find them:

freshwater habitats and around the coast

Calls and songs:

usually silent but will make grating grunting sounds when startled or at the nesting **colony**

On the move:

flies in lines with its legs outstretched; walks in shallow water, swinging its bill to sift out fish and aquatic bugs; often in flocks of 30 or more birds

What they eat:

fish, aquatic bugs, shrimp, snails, worms, leeches

Nest:

platform, in a mixed colony with herons in trees

Eggs, chicks and childcare:

1–4 olive eggs with dark marks; parents rotate the **incubation** duties and take turns feeding the kids

Spends the winter:

in Florida

SAW IT!

STAN'S COOL STUFF

The Roseate Spoonbill was devastated in the 1800s from hunters seeking its wing feathers. These were used in women's hats and fans. It's made a comeback, but now **habitat** destruction is limiting its numbers. This unusual pink bird is related to ibises (pg. 209).

Laughing Gull

Look for the black head "hood"

What to look for:
black head "**hood**" with a white neck, chest and belly, gray wings with black wing tips, and orange bill; winter **plumage** head is gray-and-white with a black bill

Where to find them:
along the coasts, freshwater and saltwater sites

Calls and songs:
a loud series of calls that sound like laughter; male tosses his head back and calls to attract a mate

On the move:
almost always in groups, moving from one water **habitat** to another

What they eat:
fish, insects on land and in the water

Nest:
ground nest, lined with grass, sticks and rocks; nests in a marsh in a large **colony**

Eggs, chicks and childcare:
2–4 olive eggs with brown marks; parents sit on the eggs and **regurgitate** food to feed the young

Spends the winter:
in southern Florida and along the coasts

REAL QUICK

Size
16–17"

Nest
GROUND

Feeder
NONE

year-round
winter

SAW IT!

STAN'S COOL STUFF

It takes this gull a few years to get adult plumage. During the first year, the young start out mostly brown-and-gray. They look like adults during the second year, but they don't have an all-black head "hood." Juveniles get the breeding plumage in the third year.

Ring-billed Gull

Look for the black ring on the bill

What to look for:

white gull with gray wings and a yellow bill with a black ring near the tip; winter **plumage** has speckles on the head and neck

Where you'll find them:

shores of large lakes and rivers; often at garbage dumps and parking lots

Calls and songs:

calls out a wide variety of loud, rising squawks and squeals—classic gull sounds

On the move:

strong flight with constant wing flaps

What they eat:

insects and fish; it also picks through garbage, scavenging for other food

Nest:

ground; defends a small area around it

Eggs, chicks and childcare:

2–4 off-white eggs with brown marks; Mom and Dad take turns incubating the eggs and feeding their young

Spends the winter:

in Florida, other southern states and Mexico

REAL QUICK

Size
18-20"

Nest
GROUND

Feeder
NONE

winter

SAW IT!

STAN'S COOL STUFF

This is one of the most common gulls in the country. Hundreds of these birds often flock together. The ring on the bill appears after the first winter. In the fall of the first three years, the birds obtain a different plumage. In the third year, they attain adult plumage.

Cattle Egret

Look for the light orange crest

What to look for:
stocky white bird with a large round head, a light orange crest, chest and back, and a reddish-orange bill and legs

Where you'll find them:
in pastures, hunting insects at cow and horse pies; attracted to sites of field fires to hunt newly exposed insects and small animals

Calls and songs:
repeats a raspy **call** over and over

On the move:
almost always in small groups of 3–5; in flight, holds its head near its body, bending its neck

What they eat:
insects, small mammals, fish and frogs

Nest:
platform; Mom and Dad build it

Eggs, chicks and childcare:
2–5 light blue-green eggs; Mom and Dad take turns incubating and feeding the young

Spends the winter:
many don't **migrate**; stays in the southern half of Florida year-round, moving around to find food

REAL QUICK

Size
18–22"

Nest
PLATFORM

Feeder
NONE

year-round
summer

SAW IT!

STAN'S COOL STUFF

This egret is from Africa. It came to South America around 1880 and reached Florida in the 1940s. To hunt, it wiggles its neck back and forth and from side to side while holding its head still. Then it stabs at **prey** and tosses it to the back of its mouth in a quick move.

Snowy Egret

Look for the bright yellow feet

What to look for:
all-white egret with a black bill and legs, bright yellow feet, and long feather plumes on the head, neck and back; yellow patch at the base of the bill

Where you'll find them:
in wetlands and often with other egrets

Calls and songs:
usually silent; when startled, gives a loud, raspy, nasal **call** as it flies away

On the move:
flies with its neck in an S shape and legs trailing

What they eat:
aquatic insects and small fish

Nest:
platform, in a **colony** that may have up to several hundred nests; nests are low in shrubs that are 5–10 feet tall or are on the ground, usually mixed among other egret and heron nests

Eggs, chicks and childcare:
3–5 light blue-green eggs; parents alternate sitting on the eggs and feeding the **hatchlings**

Spends the winter:
in Florida and other Gulf Coast states

REAL QUICK

Size
22–26"

Nest
PLATFORM

Feeder
NONE

year-round
summer

SAW IT!

STAN'S COOL STUFF

The Snowy Egret was hunted to near extinction in the late 1800s for its handsome, long feather plumes. It hunts actively for **prey**, moving around quickly in the water. It uses its feet to stir up small fish and aquatic insects, which it swiftly snaps up to eat.

White Ibis

Look for the long, down-curving bill

JUVENILE

What to look for:
white bird with a long, down-curving orange-to-red bill, pink skin on the face, pink legs, and black wing tips, seen only in flight; juvenile **plumage** is brown-and-white for the first two years

Where you'll find them:
in freshwater and saltwater habitats, but it prefers places with fresh water

Calls and songs:
just makes short grunts at the nesting **colony**

On the move:
flies in groups of 30 or more birds

What they eat:
aquatic bugs, crayfish and other **crustaceans**, fish

Nest:
platform, in a large colony; builds a well-made nest with sticks

Eggs, chicks and childcare:
2–3 light blue eggs with dark marks; Mom and Dad share **incubation** duty and feed the young

Spends the winter:
in Florida and other Gulf Coast states; most don't migrate out of Florida

REAL QUICK

Size
23–27"

Nest
PLATFORM

Feeder
NONE

year-round
summer

SAW IT!

STAN'S COOL STUFF

The White Ibis is more common in Florida than in other states. They are most common in southern Florida. Colonies with over 30,000 birds have been reported. Males are larger than females and have longer bills. Juveniles are brown, unlike the adults.

Great Egret

Look for the long, thin white neck

What to look for:
tall and thin white egret with a long neck, long legs and a long, pointed yellow bill

Where you'll find them:
shallow wetlands, ponds and lakes

Calls and songs:
gives a loud, dry croak if disturbed or when it squabbles for a nest site at the **colony**

On the move:
holds its neck in an S shape during flight; slowly stalks in shallow water, looking for fish to spear with its sharp bill

What they eat:
small fish, aquatic insects, frogs and crayfish

Nest:
platform, in a colony of up to 100 birds

Eggs, chicks and childcare:
2–3 light blue eggs; Mom and Dad sit on the eggs and give food to the **hatchlings**

Spends the winter:
in Florida and other southern states, Mexico and Central America

REAL QUICK

Size
36–40"

Nest
PLATFORM

Feeder
NONE

year-round

SAW IT!

STAN'S COOL STUFF

From the 1800s to the early 1900s, the Great Egret was hunted to near extinction for its beautiful long plumes, which were used to decorate women's hats. The plumes grow near the tail during the breeding season. Today, the egret is a protected bird.

American White Pelican

Look for the enormous bill

What to look for:
large white bird with black wing tips and a huge bright yellow or orange bill

Where you'll find them:
in small and large groups on lakes

Calls and songs:
usually silent but will give short grunts at the nesting **colony**

On the move:
groups fly in a large V, often gliding with long wings (up to 9 feet across), then all flapping together; large flocks swirl on columns of rising warm air (**thermals**) on warm summer days

What they eat:
scoops of fish

Nest:
ground nest (it's more like a scraped depression rimmed with dirt), in a colony

Eggs, chicks and childcare:
1–3 white eggs; parents take turns sitting on the eggs and feeding the kiddies

Spends the winter:
in Florida, other Gulf Coast states and Mexico

REAL QUICK

Size
60–64"

Nest
GROUND

Feeder
NONE

migration
winter

SAW IT!

STAN'S COOL STUFF

This pelican doesn't dive to catch fish. Instead, a group swims and dips their bills, all at the same time, into the water to scoop up fish. Breeding adults usually grow a large, flat plate on the middle of the upper bill. The plate drops off the bill after the eggs hatch.

American Goldfinch

Look for the black forehead

MALE

FEMALE

What to look for:

bright canary-yellow bird with a black forehead, wings and tail; female is olive-yellow and lacks a black forehead; winter male resembles the female

Where you'll find them:

open fields, scrubby areas, woodlands, backyards

Calls and songs:

male sings a pleasant high-pitched song; gives **twitter** calls during flight

On the move:

appears roller-coaster-like in flight

What they eat:

loves seeds and insects; comes to seed (especially thistle) feeders

Nest:

cup; builds its nest in late summer and lines the cup with the soft, silky down from wild thistle

Eggs, chicks and childcare:

4–6 pale blue eggs; Mom incubates the eggs and Dad pitches in to help her feed the babies

Spends the winter:

in Florida, starting in November

REAL QUICK

Size
5"

Nest
CUP

Feeder
TUBE OR HOPPER

winter

SAW IT!

STAN'S COOL STUFF

The American Goldfinch is often called Wild Canary due to its canary-colored **plumage**. This cute little feeder bird is almost always in small flocks, visiting thistle tube feeders that offer Nyjer seed. Flocks of up to 20 individuals move around to find food.

Baltimore Oriole

Look for the gray-brown wings

What to look for:

pale yellow bird with orange tones and gray-brown wings with white wing bars

Where you'll find them:

parks, yards and forests; in treetops, where it feeds on caterpillars

Calls and songs:

a fantastic songster, singing loudly; often heard before it is seen

On the move:

often returns to the same area year after year

What they eat:

insects, fruit and **nectar**; comes to nectar, orange half and grape jelly feeders

Nest:

pendulous; an interesting nest that looks like a sock hanging from an outer branch of a tall tree

Eggs, chicks and childcare:

4–5 bluish eggs with brown marks; Mom sits on the eggs; Mom and Dad do the childcare

Spends the winter:

flies to the southern half of Florida; also goes to Mexico, Central America and South America

REAL QUICK

Size
7–8"

Nest
PENDULOUS

Feeder
NECTAR

migration
winter

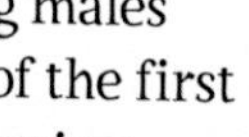

STAN'S COOL STUFF

Orioles visit feeders that offer sugar water (nectar), orange halves or grape jelly. Parents bring their young to feeders. Young males look like females for the first 1½ years. Orioles are some of the first birds to arrive in winter and some of the last to leave in spring.

Eastern Meadowlark

Look for the V-shaped black necklace

What to look for:

robin-shaped bird with a short tail, a yellow chest and belly, and a V-shaped black **necklace**; white outer tail feathers, usually seen when flying away

Where to find them:

meadows, open grassy country, roadsides

Calls and songs:

sings a wonderful flute-like, clear whistling song

On the move:

if you move toward it when it's perching on a fence post, it will quickly dive into tall grass

What they eat:

insects and seeds

Nest:

cup on the ground in dense **cover**; Mom builds the nest by herself

Eggs, chicks and childcare:

3–5 white eggs with brown marks; Mom sits on the eggs, but both parents feed the **hatchlings**; pairs have 2 broods per year

Spends the winter:

in Florida and other southern states, Mexico and Central America

REAL QUICK

Size
9"

Nest
CUP

Feeder
NONE

year-round

SAW IT!

STAN'S COOL STUFF

The Eastern Meadowlark is a bird that likes to live in meadows. Meadowlarks are ground-dwelling songbirds that sing while they fly. They are members of the blackbird family, which makes them relatives of orioles and grackles.

BIRD FOOD FUN FOR THE FAMILY

If you and your family like to do fun projects together, making your own bird food and bird-feeding items might be just the right ones to try. Chances are good that you already have most of the ingredients at home to make delicious and nutritious treats for your wild bird friends.

You'll be doing these projects in the kitchen, so show your mom or dad the following sections. They're written specifically with the whole family in mind. For example, you may need to check with a parent or guardian for help with such tasks as grocery shopping, stovetop cooking or food preparation, like cutting up fresh fruit.

STARTER SNACKS AND FRUIT TREATS

You can start by offering some food that's already in your kitchen. Peanut butter attracts a lot of birds! Simply use a spatula to smear some on the bark of a nearby tree where you can watch it from a window. Or use a piece of firewood: prop it up or hang it with a rope and slather it with peanut butter—then watch the birds go wild.

To offer treats like raisins, dates and currents, place them outside in a nonbreakable small bowl with a few holes drilled in the bottom for drainage. Waxwings, robins, catbirds and many other birds love small dried fruit, and some will be flying in shortly to get some.

Putting out fresh fruit, such as apples and oranges, is another great way to attract bright and colorful birds to your yard. Cut these into small, manageable pieces, and offer the snacks on the tray of a feeder.

Another cool way to serve an orange is to cut one in half and place the halves sunny-side up on a feeder or branch. This arrangement allows birds to easily feast on the sweet fruit contained inside the rind. Sometimes it's best to impale the orange half on a nail to stop it from rolling away.

Plain and unsalted nuts, especially peanuts, pecans and walnuts, make wonderful treats for birds. Simply add these to a feeder tray with seeds or place them in a tube feeder for nuts.

EASY BIRD FOOD RECIPES

Preparing bird food of any kind shows that you care about the birds in your backyard. Now, are you ready to try making some recipes? Below are just a few suggestions. You can find much more online.

Sweet Homemade Nectar

Nectar is a superb food for many birds. Studies of nectar from flowers have shown that the average flower is 25 percent sucrose. Sucrose is a simple sugar, so to make the correct strength of homemade nectar (sugar water), mix a ratio of 1 part sugar to 4 parts water. You'll discover that hummingbirds, orioles and woodpeckers will thoroughly enjoy the sweet drink that you made.

INGREDIENTS
¼ cup granulated white sugar
1 cup warm water

DIRECTIONS: Add the sugar to the water and stir to dissolve. If you prefer, you can boil the water first so the sugar dissolves more quickly. Cool to room temperature before filling your feeder. Store any extra in the refrigerator or freezer.

NOTES: Never substitute brown sugar or honey for the white sugar. Also, there is no need to add red food coloring because the birds will be attracted to any amount of red on any part of your **nectar** feeder.

Birds-Go-Wild Spread

INGREDIENTS
½ cup raisins
½ cup granola
½ cup oatmeal
½ cup Cheerios
16-ounce jar smooth peanut butter

DIRECTIONS: Mix dry ingredients in a large mixing bowl. Warm the peanut butter in a microwave or place the jar in warm water to soften. Scoop out the softened peanut butter, and mix well with dry ingredients until smooth.

Spread on tree bark or smear a few dollops on the tray of a feeder.

Love-It-Nutty Butter

INGREDIENTS
2 cups shelled peanuts, unsalted
2 cups shelled walnuts, unsalted
¼ cup raisins
3–5 tablespoons coconut oil or other vegetable oil

DIRECTIONS: Toss dry ingredients into a food processor. Start blending. Add oil until the mixture reaches a smooth, thick consistency. Store in refrigerator.

Smear on a wooden board with grooves or spread on tree bark.

MAKE YOUR OWN SUET

You and your family can make outstanding **suet** recipes at home, too. Suet is animal fat, often from cows, and there are several convenient ways to get it for your recipes.

A quick way is to purchase plain suet cakes. In store-bought suet, the fat has already been melted down (**rendered**). A cheaper way might be to buy fat trimmings in bulk from your local butcher or large amounts of **lard** at your grocery store. A clever way to get rendered fat from your own kitchen is for an adult to pour fat drippings from cooked bacon, pork and beef into an empty, clean can. When the fat has cooled and solidified, cover and refrigerate to save for future use.

Easy-Peasy Suet

INGREDIENTS
1 cup solidified fat of your choice
1 cup chunky peanut butter
3 cups ground cornmeal
1 cup white flour
1 cup black oil sunflower seeds or peanuts

DIRECTIONS: In a large pot, melt the fat over low heat. Do not heat quickly or the fat might burn. Strain the fat through a **cheesecloth** to remove any chunks, and then pour the liquid back into the pot.

Add the peanut butter to the fat. Stir over low heat until the mixture melts and consistency is smooth. Remove from heat. Add the cornmeal and flour, and mix until stiff. Add the sunflower seeds or peanuts, and mix thoroughly.

Pour into a mold or container. With a spatula, spread out the mixture and smooth the top. Cool completely, then cut into squares. Store in freezer.

Simply Super Suet

INGREDIENTS
2 cups **suet** or **lard**
1 cup peanut butter
2 cups yellow cornmeal
2 cups cracked corn
1 cup black oil sunflower seeds

DIRECTIONS: In a large pot, melt the suet or lard over low heat. Add the peanut butter, stirring until melted and well mixed. Add remaining ingredients, and mix.

Pour into baking pans or forms and allow to cool. Cut into chunks or shapes. Store in freezer.

YUMMY BIRD-FEEDING PROJECTS

Bird-feeding projects are super activities for families, and they can be a big hit at special occasions, such as birthday parties. These very attractive ornaments and feeders also make unique gifts for the holidays and family celebrations.

Birdseed Ornaments

INGREDIENTS
cookie cutters in any shape
nonstick cooking spray
½ cup water
3 tablespoons white corn syrup
2½ teaspoons unflavored gelatin
¾ cup white flour
4 cups black oil sunflower seeds
10- to 12-inch pieces of string or **jute** twine

DIRECTIONS: Place the cookie cutters on wax paper and spray with nonstick cooking spray. Set aside.

In a saucepan, bring the water and corn syrup to a boil. Reduce heat and stir in gelatin until completely mixed. Do not overcook.

Transfer the hot liquid to a bowl. Add the flour, and mix until smooth. Add the sunflower seeds, and mix well. Mixture will now be thick.

Use a spatula to fill each cookie cutter. Be sure to press the seeds into all parts of the shapes. Roll any extra mixture into balls. Poke one hole through each shape and each ball with a pencil or similar object.

When cooled, pop out the ornaments from the cookie cutters. Thread a length of string or twine through each hole, and tie the ends to form a loop. Loop each of your ornaments over nearby branches, and watch the birds come to feast!

Pinecone Birdseed Feeders

Try your hand at making this fabulous little bird feeder from an ordinary pinecone. It's fun and easy, and everyone in your family can make their own.

INGREDIENTS (per person)
1 pinecone
10- to 12-inch piece of string or **jute** twine
peanut butter
birdseed

DIRECTIONS: Tie a piece of string or twine to a pinecone. Roll the cone in peanut butter, filling the spaces between the "petals" (bracts) and coating the entire surface. Then roll the cone in birdseed until the seeds completely cover the peanut butter.

Hang the feeder outside where you can see the birds feeding on it, and enjoy the show!

MORE ACTIVITIES FOR THE BIRD-MINDED

Nothing brings family and friends closer together than a shared interest. Birding and backyard bird feeding are enjoyable, year-round activities that many find appealing. Here are some things to do that are not only fun for everyone but also supportive for the birds.

Help Birds Build Their Nests

A thoughtful way for the entire family to work together with birds during spring is to put out a variety of soft and flexible natural items to help birds build their nests.

First, gather some everyday materials around your home that birds will use. Here are some excellent items to offer:

- Yarn, cut into 6-inch-long pieces.
- Fabric from an old, clean T-shirt, cut into 6-inch-long strips.
- Cotton batting (used for handicrafts).
- Fuzzy pet hair from a brush.
- Fluffy dryer lint from the dryer filter.

Next, place your materials into an unused, clean suet cage. Be sure to let the ends of the yarn and fabric strips hang out, and don't pack the material in tightly. The birds need to be able to take out the items easily.

Hang the cage by a short chain from a tree in early spring, when the birds are starting to construct their nests. And then, wait...

Soon, birds will be flying back and forth to the materials and choosing their favorites. It's a delight to see birds making use of your nesting contributions. Not only have you assisted the bird parents, but you've also helped them provide a comfy home for their families. Good job!

Make a Bird Watch List

Making a watch list on **poster board** of the birds that have visited your yard is a handicraft project that the whole family will enjoy. You can decorate the poster any way you like, but it's awesome to show pictures of the birds you've spotted and write notes about the sightings.

Each time you see a new species in your yard, mark it on the poster with the date and time of day. Attach it to the refrigerator, or put it in another prominent place where it's easy for everyone in the family to see and add their updates.

Your watch list is also a valuable way to track the arrival of the first hummingbirds and orioles in your area each spring. If you create a new watch list each year, it could reveal trends in the arrival dates. This information would be of interest not only to your family and friends, but also to your teachers and local birding organizations.

Save the Birds with Hawk Cutouts

Another fun and important project is to make hawk cutouts to attach to your windows. These items will help prevent birds from flying into sheets of glass at your home.

In-flight window strikes are the number one killer of our wild bird friends. Window reflections of the sky, trees and other natural features in your yard create the illusion to birds that the flight path is clear. When birds see forms of predator birds in the reflections, they will turn away and take another route.

Various web pages show outlines (**silhouettes**) of hawks that you can print and cut out. Check the possibilities, and then pick your favorites.

Tape the cutouts to any large picture windows, as well as other windows and doors with clear glass. This preventive action will greatly reduce the risk of birds crashing headfirst into glass. Then give yourself a high five for helping to save them.

Build Your Very Own Birdhouse

A first-rate project for kids and adults to do together is to construct a birdhouse. Building plans are available online for different kinds of birdhouses for different kinds of birds. Give them a once-over and pick one that you like best for the birds you want nesting nearby.

The instructions online will help you select the right kind of wood and show you how to cut it to the right sizes. Most importantly, the plans will provide the correct size of the entrance hole for the bird, along with how-to instructions for making it. Most birdhouse projects require hand and power tools, so be sure to work with a parent or guardian.

You might even want to make multiple birdhouses with your extended family or your neighbors. With everyone doing different tasks, your team can turn out a bluebird box, a wren box, a robin platform and more!

Create a Bird-Friendly Yard

There is no better way to support the birds in your area than to plant bird-friendly flowers, bushes and trees. There are many varieties of these plants, making it easy to choose some that will be ideal for your yard.

Planting perennials that bloom large and showy flowers each year is an outstanding way to feed hummingbirds. Many shrubs produce attractive **nectar**-filled flowers and then, later in the summer, edible fruit, which the birds love. Numerous tree species offer berries and nuts—foods the birds depend on in late fall.

A yard with grass alone just isn't a friendly **habitat** for birds, so sit down with your family and think about putting in a flower garden or adorning your yard with some shrubs and trees. Soon afterward, you'll be hearing the sweet chirping of birds and a rich repertoire of **birdsong** all around you.

Take a Birding Trip

Everyone loves a good time! For a fun family outing, plan a birding trip to a local park, state park or national wildlife refuge. In spring, you'll be rewarded with migrating warblers. During summer, all of the nesting birds will be feeding babies. In fall, waterfowl will be super-active. Even in winter, there are many amazing birds to see.

Your local nature center is another good place to see birds. Oftentimes nature centers have bird feeders set up to attract birds. Stop in after school or early on Saturday mornings to see what comes to the feeders.

The shores along the Atlantic Ocean and the Gulf of Mexico are fantastic places where other incredible birds gather. Pack a picnic lunch and head out with your family to enjoy both the outdoors and the birds that don't hang around feeders. Cormorants, ospreys and gulls are just some of the cool birds that spend their time around the water.

Practice Good Birding

Finding a stray feather or an empty bird nest is exciting when you and your family are sharing time in nature. Examining these wonders and making a sketch or taking photos are always fun educational opportunities. However, everyone should be aware that collecting, possessing or owning wild bird feathers, nests, and even bird eggs is not permitted under federal law.

It may seem silly that a lost feather or vacant bird nest needs protecting, but very important laws stop people from buying, selling and trading these items. In the past, a lively market for feathers, bird nests, and also eggs led to widespread killing of birds, some to near extinction. To prevent from this happening again, strong laws were passed to safeguard all of our bird species.

So enjoy seeing, studying and learning about birds, but please don't take any feathers, nests or eggs with you out of their natural environment. Leave them just as you found them, and perhaps someone else will also get the opportunity to benefit from studying them.

CITIZEN SCIENCE PROJECTS

I can't think of a more exciting way to learn about birds and expand the birding experience than to take part in a citizen science project. If you are unfamiliar with citizen science projects, they are sponsored by organizations in which citizens like yourself can contribute in a meaningful way to actual scientific projects right from your own home! Most projects don't take much time and can be fun family activities, with everyone sharing what they learned about birds.

There are simple citizen projects that might have you just count the birds that come to your feeders. Others are more complex and involve more time, effort, and perhaps a little traveling. Either way, I'm sure you can find an enjoyable and educational citizen project that will be a perfect fit for your family. Give it a try!

Here are some popular projects and resources for you to explore:

How to find citizen science projects, from birds to mammals.

www.birds.cornell.edu/citscitoolkit/projects/find

The very well-known Christmas Bird Count winter census, FeederWatch and more.

www.birds.cornell.edu/page.aspx?pid=1664

Hummingbird migration.

https://journeynorth.org/tm/humm/AboutSpring.html

Finding and counting nesting birds.

https://nestwatch.org

General citizen science projects for counting birds.

www.birdwatchingdaily.com/featured-stories/year-round-citizen-science-projects

General overview of many citizen science projects.

https://www.americanornithology.org/content/citizen-science-projects

American Kestrel nesting and population study.

https://kestrel.peregrinefund.org

LEARNING ABOUT BIRDING ON THE INTERNET

Birding online is another fine way to discover more information about birds—plus it's a terrific way to spend time during rainy summer days and winter evenings after sunset. So check out the websites below, and be sure to share with your family and friends the fabulous things you've learned about birds.

eBird

https://ebird.org/home

American Birding Association: Young Birders

https://www.aba.org/aba-young-birders/

Cornell Lab of Ornithology

www.birds.cornell.edu/Page.aspx?pid=1478

Author Stan Tekiela's website

www.naturesmart.com

In addition, online birding groups can be of valuable assistance to you as well. Facebook has many pages dedicated to specific areas of the state and the birds that live there. These sites are an excellent, real-time resource that will help you spot birds in your region. Consider joining a Facebook group.

GLOSSARY

birdsong: A series of musical notes that a bird strings together in a pleasing melody. Also called a song.

brood: A family of bird brothers and sisters that hatched at around the same time.

brood parasites: Birds that don't nest, incubate or raise families, such as Brown-headed Cowbirds (pg. 21). See *host*.

call: A nonmusical sound, often a single note, that is repeated.

carrion: A dead and often rotting animal's body, or carcass, that is an important food for many other animals, including birds.

cheesecloth: A loosely woven cotton cloth that is used primarily to wrap cheese. It is also used to strain particles from liquids.

colony: A group of birds nesting together in the same area. The size of a colony can range from two pairs to hundreds of birds.

coniferous: A tree or shrub that has evergreen, needle-like leaves and that produces cones.

cotton batting: A light, soft cotton material, often used to stuff quilts.

cover: A dense area of trees or shrubs where birds nest or hide.

crustaceans: A large, mainly aquatic group of critters, such as crayfish, crabs and shrimp.

deciduous: A tree or shrub that sheds its leaves every year.

display: An attention-getting behavior of birds to impress and attract a mate, or to draw predators away from the nest. A display may include dramatic movements in flight or on the ground.

epaulets: Decorative color patches on the shoulders of a bird, as seen in male Red-winged Blackbirds (pg. 25).

excavate: To dig or carefully remove wood or dirt, creating a cavity, hole or tunnel.

fencerow: An overgrown strip of land or uncultivated vegetation along a fence.

fledge: The process of developing flight feathers and leaving the nest.

flock: A group of the same bird species or a gathering of mixed species of birds. Flocks range from a pair of birds to upwards of 10,000 individuals.

habitat: The natural home or environment of a bird.

hatchlings: Baby birds that have recently emerged from their eggs. See *nestlings*.

hood: The markings on the head of a bird, resembling a hood.

horns: A tuft or collection of feathers, usually on top of a bird's head, resembling horns.

host: A bird species that takes care of the eggs and babies of other bird species. See *brood parasites*.

incubation: The process of sitting on bird eggs in the nest to keep them warm until they hatch.

iridescent: A luminous, or bright, quality of feathers, with colors seeming to change when viewed from different angles.

jute: A string of rough fibers made from plants.

lard: Fat from mammals, such as cows and pigs.

lichen: A unique partnership of plant life and fungi growing together and looking and acting as one organism.

lore: The area on each side of a bird's face between the eye and the base of the bill.

migrate: The regular, predictable pattern of seasonal movement by some birds from one region to another, especially to escape winter.

mollusks: Soft-bodied critters that lack a backbone (invertebrate), such as snails, slugs, clams, oysters and mussels.

molt: The process of dropping old, worn-out feathers and replacing them with new feathers, usually only one feather at a time.

morph: A different color from the normal color of a bird. Morphs also sometimes occur in mammals, reptiles, amphibians and insects.

mute: The inability to make or produce audible sounds. The Turkey Vulture (pg. 41), for example, is mostly mute.

necklace: The markings around the neck of a bird, as seen in the Eastern Meadowlark (pg. 219).

nectar: A sugar and water solution usually consisting of about 25 percent sucrose and 75 percent water, usually found in flowers.

nestlings: Young birds that have not yet left the nest. See *hatchlings*.

pair bond: The relationship between a male and female bird during the mating season.

plumage: The collective set of feathers on a bird at any given time.

poster board: A stiff cardboard that is used for displaying information.

prey: Any critter that is hunted and killed by another for food.

raptor: A flesh-eating bird of prey that hunts and kills for food. Hawks, eagles, ospreys, falcons, owls and vultures are raptors. See *prey*.

refraction: The bending of light.

regurgitate: The process of bringing swallowed food up again to the mouth to feed young birds.

rendered: Animal fat that has been reduced or melted down by heating in order to make it pure.

silhouettes: Dark shapes or outlines against a lighter background.

speculum: A patch of bright feathers on some birds, such as ducks, found on the wings.

squab: A young pigeon or dove, usually still in the nest. See *nestlings*.

suet: Animal fat, usually beef, that has been heated and made into cakes to feed birds. See *rendered*.

thermals: A column of upward-moving warm air caused by the sun warming the earth. Raptors and other birds gain altitude during flight by "riding" on thermals.

trachea: A large tubelike organ that allows air to pass between the lung and the mouth of a bird. Also called a windpipe.

tree sap: The watery liquid that moves up and down within the circulatory system of a tree, carrying nutrients throughout.

trill: A fluttering or repeated series of similar-sounding musical notes given by some birds.

twitter: A high-pitched call of a bird. See *call*.

ultraviolet light: A kind of light that is visible to birds and insects but unseen by people.

vegetation: Any plants, especially those found growing in a particular habitat.

waterfowl: A group of similar birds with a strong connection to water. Ducks, geese, swans and others, including American Coots (pg. 31), are examples of waterfowl.

CHECKLIST/INDEX BY SPECIES

Use the circles to checkmark the birds you've seen.

ABOUT THE AUTHOR

Naturalist, wildlife photographer and writer Stan Tekiela is the originator of the popular state-specific field guide series that includes *Birds of Florida Field Guide*. Stan has authored more than 190 educational books, including field guides, quick guides, nature books, children's books, playing cards and more, presenting many species of animals and plants.

With a Bachelor of Science degree in Natural History from the University of Minnesota and as an active professional naturalist for more than 30 years, Stan studies and photographs wildlife throughout the United States and Canada. He has received various national and regional awards for his books and photographs. Also a well-known columnist and radio personality, his syndicated column appears in more than 25 newspapers, and his wildlife programs are broadcast on a number of Midwest radio stations. Stan can be followed on Facebook and Twitter. He can be contacted via www.naturesmart.com.